Jockey Hollow

Celebrate History!

I hope you enjoy the book,

Rosalie Lauerman

Jockey Hollow

WHERE A FORGOTTEN ARMY PERSEVERED TO WIN AMERICA'S FREEDOM

Rosalie Lauerman

To my family:
My husband Dave;
Our son, Kurt, his wife, Tricia,
and their children, Thomas, and Charlotte;
Our son, Tom, his wife, Shannon,
and their children, Marcella, and Felix

Cover Image: Washington Leading the Continental Army to Valley Forge winter camp.
Courtesy of North Wind Picture Archives Color. This image and a few other images in
this book show an artist's depiction of the soldiers' hardships at Valley Forge. The
images also illustrate conditions at Jockey Hollow, as they were no better two years later.

Published by Rosalie Lauerman
Copyright: (c) 2015 Rosalie Lauerman
All rights reserved
rosalielauerman@msn.com
ISBN: 978-0-692-50783-4

Acknowledgments

I wish to thank the following individuals who helped bring this book to life. Marcia Hoehne for her untiring advice and enthusiasm, Dr. Jude Pfister for sharing his knowledge and understanding of Jockey Hollow, Dr. Sarah Minegar for thoroughly researching sources, David Gruol Photography for remarkable Jockey Hollow photographs, Carol Gaskin for a perceptive edit, and Lilian Rosenstreich for her creative designs. Most of all I am forever grateful to my family and friends for encouraging me and allowing me to live in the 18th century.

Contents

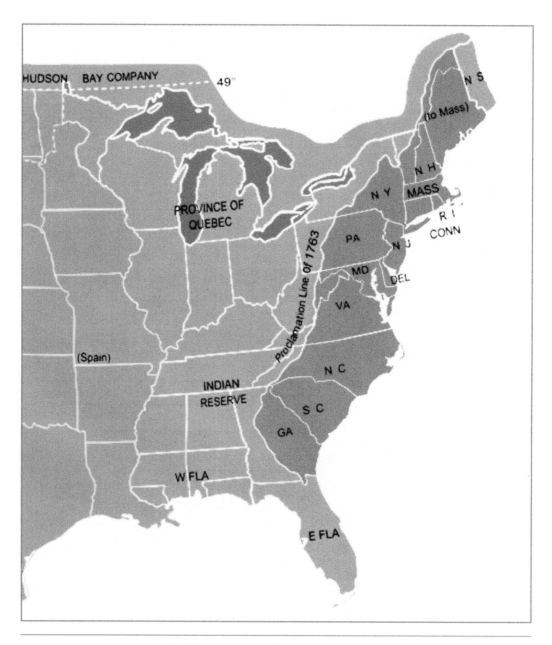

AMERICA'S TERRITORIAL BOUNDARIES BEFORE THE REVOLUTION.
GREAT BRITAIN CLAIMED THE RED AND PINK SECTIONS. SPAIN CLAIMED THE
ORANGE AREA. MOST AMERICAN COLONISTS SETTLED ALONG THE COASTLINE,
THE RED AREA OF THE MAP. THE THIRTEEN ORIGINAL COLONIES WERE NEW
HAMPSHIRE, MASSACHUSETTS, CONNECTICUT, RHODE ISLAND, NEW YORK,
PENNSYLVANIA, NEW JERSEY, MARYLAND, DELAWARE, VIRGINIA, NORTH
CAROLINA, SOUTH CAROLINA, AND GEORGIA.

Introduction

You know about Valley Forge, right? That's the Revolutionary War camp in Pennsylvania where General George Washington's army endured horrific conditions during the winter of 1777-78. Some say it's where America came closest to losing the war for freedom from Great Britain. Others describe it as the lowest point of the American Revolution and "the worst of times."

But wait! You might decide that conditions were even worse and the war's outcome even more precarious during the encampments of 1779-1782 in a wilderness called Jockey Hollow, near Morristown, New Jersey.

This is Jockey Hollow's story. Meet the heroic Jockey Hollow soldiers—beaten up and worn down by five years of fighting the world's strongest army. Hear their stories. Witness their battles. Be inspired by their perseverance. Read how these extreme underdogs stepped back from the brink of mutiny to win their country's freedom.

ONE

Weather

"[We] reached this wilderness, about three miles from Morristown, where we are to build log huts for winter quarters. Our baggage is [left] in the rear, for want of wagons to transport it. The snow on the ground is about two feet deep, and the weather extremely cold; the soldiers are [without] both tents and blankets, and some of them are actually barefooted and almost naked."

This was Dr. James Thacher's journal entry for December 14, 1779, the day he arrived at Jockey Hollow. He was a twenty-five-year-old surgeon in the **Continental Army** during the American Revolution, and his journal survived to become a reliable eyewitness account of the war.

According to Thacher, "Our lodging . . . last

The American army that battled the British during the Revolution was called the Continental Army. Most of the soldiers were born and raised on the American continent, and they fought for the rights of all who lived in the thirteen colonies.

night was on the frozen ground. Those officers who have the privilege of a horse can always have a blanket at hand. Having removed the snow, we [the officers] wrapped ourselves in great coats, spread our blankets on the ground, and lay down by the side of each other five or six together, with large fires at our feet. . . . We can scarcely keep from freezing."

Days later the baggage wagons finally plowed through the snow, bringing tents and supplies. The men struggled to pitch their tents on the rock-solid frozen ground, but at least each man now had a blanket and a bundle of straw for a mattress.

In colonial times, armies didn't fight in winter. Instead, they spent the harsh winter months in camps, training and drilling. The British, the enemy, moved to their winter camp at New York in November 1779. General George Washington chose Jockey Hollow for the Continental Army's winter camp.

Washington had worked as a land surveyor when he was sixteen years old. Because of that experience, he could see that Jockey Hollow's natural resources would be useful to the army. The thirty-mile-long, hook-shaped Watchung Mountains sheltered Jockey Hollow on three sides. They were steep, rugged, and thickly forested. A forbidding marsh, called the Great Swamp, blocked travel at the foot of the mountains. These natural barriers protected the camp from surprise attacks.

Washington also used the mountaintops to call out the militia, or part-time soldiers. If the enemy approached, lookouts on the mountain ridges would fire the cannon and ignite signal beacons. When militiamen heard the booming cannon and saw the flaming, smoking beacons, they'd drop everything and report for battle.

Jockey Hollow offered even more. Several iron mines operated northwest of nearby Morristown. Local furnaces forged iron ore into cannonballs, shot, and other hardware for the army. Jacob Ford, a successful iron mine owner and businessman, built a powder mill to manufacture gunpowder for the Continental Army. Fertile farmland for growing produce and grazing livestock surrounded Jockey Hollow. The plentiful harvests fed the army—sometimes. Jockey Hollow's dense forest became logs for huts and wood for fires. And Henry Wick, an apple farmer, loaned his 1,400-acre farm to the Continental Army for its camp.

Over time, Washington found Jockey Hollow so ideal that he kept some troops there for the remainder of the war.

Washington and his aides arrived in Morristown on December 1, 1779. A fierce storm spewing hail and snow raged all day and night. It was the fifth snowfall of the season, with twenty days to go before winter officially began.

JOCKEY HOLLOW AREA. THE BLUE DOT REPRESENTS THE LOCATION OF JOCKEY HOLLOW. THE RED DOT IS THE BRITISH CAMP. ORANGE MARKINGS ARE MOUNTAIN RIDGES. ARROWS POINT TO HOBART GAP, THE BEST PASS THROUGH THE WATCHUNG MOUNTAINS.

Soldiers continued to arrive at Jockey Hollow throughout December, plodding through knee-deep snow all the way.

"Our march lasted six days," Major General Johann de Kalb wrote of his division's march from West Point, New York, to Jockey Hollow. De Kalb, an experienced German general, had joined the Continentals because he respected their spirit of independence and their right to be free. Some of his men died on that six-day march because of "the cold, the bad weather, the horrid roads, the necessity of spending the night in the open air, and our want of protection [from] snow and rain."

In all 10,800 men wintered in Jockey Hollow. Many were battle-weary veterans who'd been fighting the war for almost five years. They were half-starved, half-clothed, and freezing.

On January 2, 1780, the worst blizzard in a hundred years roared into Jockey Hollow and churned for three days. Temperatures dropped to zero and stayed there. Rivers froze almost to their bottoms. By the third day, snow had drifted as high as six feet.

Dr. Thacher described it as "one of the most tremendous snowstorms ever remembered; no man could endure its violence many minutes without danger of his life. . . . Some of the soldiers were actually covered while in their tents, and buried like sheep under the snow."

General Washington reported that snowdrifts blocked all roads to Jockey Hollow. Townspeople and soldiers worked to clear paths on the main roads. No one knows exactly how they did this. Some suggest they walked up and down the roads to pack the snow for sleds and wagons. Still, if duty called a soldier to Morristown, he'd trudge three miles on foot, through drifts as high as his head.

The fierce winter raged on for months. In February de Kalb wrote, "Ink freezes in my pen, while I am sitting close by the fire." He

REVOLUTIONARY WAR
CANNON AT A LOOKOUT
POST IN MORRISTOWN

described snow piles along the roads as high as twelve feet.

In March, an officer reported that an immense body of snow remained on the ground.

The last snowflake floated down on April 1, part of a ten-inch snowstorm.

In all, Jockey Hollow endured twenty-eight snowfalls that winter. It was the coldest, snowiest, and longest winter of the century.

De Kalb summed it up. "Those who have only been in Valley Forge and Middlebrook during the last two winters, but have not tasted the cruelties of this one, know not what it is to suffer."

And the weather wasn't the army's only problem.

Have You Heard about Lord Stirling's Signal Beacons?

Throughout history fire had been used to send instant messages; not even Paul Revere could travel at light-speed. When the British threatened to attack, the Continental Army needed a way to immediately warn citizens and summon militiamen—civilian soldiers with military training who could be called up in emergencies. So General Washington directed Lord Stirling to plan and oversee construction of a line of signal beacons that could be set afire on the highest Watchung Mountain ridges

William Alexander, born in America but called Lord Stirling because he claimed a Scottish title, was a major general in the Continental Army. He sketched detailed plans for the beacons. The soldiers built them, pyramid-shaped towers of stacked logs that stood twenty feet tall. Each beacon was built around a thirty-foot-tall sapling tree. The base of the tower was fourteen feet square and tapered to six feet square at the top. Easily ignited dry brush filled the inside of the towers.

When a lookout spotted the enemy, he'd ignite the brush and fire the cannon. One lit tower was a signal to light the others in the line. Smoking, flaming towers of fire and booming cannons called the militiamen to battle and warned the residents of a possible attack. The signal beacons served their purpose many times.

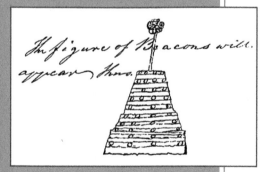

FOR MORE about the signal beacons, check out Lincoln Diamant's book, Chaining the Hudson, (New York: Carol Publishing Group, 1994), Chapter 4.

TWO

Shelter

"Since the beginning of this month, we have been busy putting up our [huts]," Major General de Kalb wrote in December 1779. "But the severe frost greatly retards our work, and does not even permit us to complete our chimneys."

The soldiers worked intensely on their huts at Jockey Hollow in spite of the interruptions caused by constant snowstorms. In fact, the extreme weather pushed them to work faster. Until they completed their log huts, the freezing men had to live in drafty tents during the harshest winter of the century.

Dr. Thacher was concerned. "The sufferings of the poor soldiers can scarcely be described. While on duty, they are unavoidably exposed to all the [hazards] of storms and severe cold."

General Nathanael Greene had planned the camp layout. Soldiers camped together in brigades, commanded by a brigadier general. A brigade consisted of one to four regiments. A colonel commanded each regiment. Greene assigned separate hillside locations for each of the eight brigades. Soldiers' huts were lined up in straight rows of eight huts across the front, three to five rows deep. Twelve soldiers lived in each hut. Officers' cabins were behind the soldiers' huts.

To build the huts, the men first cleared the snow. Then they cut down trees, stripped off branches, and sawed logs to the required lengths. In all, they cleared almost a thousand acres of oak and walnut trees.

Each log hut was fourteen feet wide, sixteen feet long, and six and a half feet high, with a packed dirt floor. The soldiers chopped notches into the ends of the logs so that the logs locked together. They didn't need nails. After the walls were built, they plugged gaps between the logs with clay or mud. Roofs were made from flat boards, shingles, and small logs. Each hut had a fireplace and twelve wooden bunk beds stacked three-high along the walls.

If a hut failed to meet standards, Greene ordered the men to tear it down and rebuild it correctly. Few needed to be rebuilt.

While working on the huts, nineteen-year-old Private Joseph Plumb Martin observed, "When digging just below the frost . . . we dug out a number of toads, that would hop off when brought to the light of day as lively as in summertime. We found by this where toads take up their winter quarters."

Most soldiers were in their huts by the end of December. After the soldiers finished their huts, they built the officers' cabins. Two to four officers occupied each building. Their cabins had windows, wood floors, and two fireplaces. But through the worst winter weather, the officers lived in tents that provided very little shelter from wind, rain, and snow.

On February 14, 1780, Dr. Thacher wrote, "We have now the satisfaction of taking possession of the log huts, just completed by our soldiers, where we shall have more comfortable accommodations."

By the end of February, everyone was sheltered.

RECONSTRUCTED
SOLDIERS' HUTS AT THE
PENNSYLVANIA LINE'S
ORIGINAL CAMPSITE IN
JOCKEY HOLLOW, NOW
PART OF MORRISTOWN
NATIONAL HISTORICAL
PARK

INTERLOCKING NOTCHED
LOGS

FIREPLACE AND
CHIMNEY OF NATIVE
STONE AND WOOD

TWELVE MEN SLEEP
IN EACH HUT ON FLAT
BOARDS WITH STRAW
FOR MATTRESSES. A
SINGLE FIREPLACE
LIGHTS AND WARMS
THE HUT, COOKS THE
SOLDIERS' MEALS, AND
DRIES THEIR CLOTHES.

During that winter, a visiting schoolmaster described the one thousand or more huts as a "log-house city." Almost eleven thousand men lived in the log-house city, making it the largest city in New Jersey.

The Grand Parade, an open field the length of four football fields, was set aside for assemblies. During the long winter, the log-house city residents assembled at the Grand Parade for daily orders, inspections, training, and drills. Their outdoor duties included patrolling, standing guard, and clearing snow. Inside the huts, soldiers cooked meals in the fireplace, mended clothes, and cleaned their muskets. On cold, dark evenings they gathered around the fireplace to play cards, checkers, dice, or darts. Some sang to music played on homemade instruments. Others read and wrote letters.

Most of the soldiers were young unmarried men without property. They had worked as apprentices, servants, or laborers. The New Englanders were farmers and tradesmen. Men who lived along the coast were fishermen. The rugged woodsmen from Pennsylvania and Maryland were hunters. Most brought their own guns. Everyone knew how to use one.

At Jockey Hollow, officers lived in huts near their soldiers. But a few senior officers stayed in private homes in Morristown. About two hundred and fifty people, mostly farmers and ironworkers, lived in Morristown in 1780. The town's sixty houses spread out from its center, an open lawn called "the green." Churches, the courthouse, an inn, and a tavern faced the green. A visiting officer's wife from Virginia described Morristown as a very pretty little village in a beautiful valley. She thought the church steeples around the green made the town look noteworthy.

Washington felt that the army's headquarters should impress visitors with the dignity and importance of the office. So he set up headquarters in the Ford mansion, one of the grandest houses in Morristown, owned by Theodosia Ford. Her husband, Jacob, a businessman in the iron industry, had died in 1777 while commanding the Morris County Militia.

Washington and his aides occupied half of the first floor and the entire second floor of the mansion. Mrs. Ford and her four children lived in two rooms on the first floor. All shared the kitchen.

Officers, guests, guards, and servants swarmed throughout the house. While the Ford children, aged eight to fifteen, loved the excitement, Mrs. Ford felt crowded. Washington, too, wished for more space.

He complained to Quartermaster Greene, "Eighteen [servants] belonging to my family and all Mrs. Fords are [crowded] together in her Kitchen and scarce one of them able to speak for the colds they have caught."

FORD MANSION
AND WASHINGTON'S
HEADQUARTERS

He ordered several outbuildings to be constructed to reduce crowding in the mansion.

Washington's Life Guard also lived on the mansion grounds in huts that they built. The Life Guard was a troop of carefully chosen men who protected the general as well as the Army's top-secret records. The Life Guard was also a top fighting unit and was often called into battle.

Martha Washington joined her husband in Morristown on December 31, 1779 and stayed for five months. Deep snow forced Martha

to travel part of the way by sleigh. While at headquarters, she helped with paperwork. Cheerfully, she planned dinners and entertainments for visiting officials. In her free time she knitted woolen socks for the soldiers and encouraged other officers' wives to join her. Warm, dry socks without holes were the greatest luxury for marching soldiers.

But Martha worried about the general's gloomy mood. Back home she admitted, "The poor General was so unhappy that it distressed me exceedingly."

FOR MORE about the soldiers at Jockey Hollow, don't miss this NJN public television video. Go to the Washington Association of New Jersey's website at www.wanj.org, select "Videos about George Washington" and choose "Morristown, Where America Survived." Enjoy the 26-minute video.

Have You Heard about the Youngest Soldier?

Richard Lord Jones joined the Continental Army when he was ten years old. At the time, Richard was told he was the youngest person on the army payroll.

In the army he learned to play the fife, a musical instrument like a flute, and served as a fifer. Fifes and drums signaled commands to the troops, such as calling them to assemble in camp or announcing a charge on the battlefield.

Richard was thirteen when he marched barefooted to Jockey Hollow in December 1779. While at Jockey Hollow, he was asked to sing a patriotic song for Martha Washington and some other visitors. After his solo Martha pressed a folded $3.00 Continental bill into his hand to thank him. He treasured the bill all his life and kept it folded just as she had folded it. After the war Richard Lord Jones settled on a farm near New Albany, Indiana. He lived to be eighty-five. His grave is marked, "Revolutionary War, Ten Year Old Fifer."

THE STATE HOUSE IN PHILADELPHIA (NOW CALLED INDEPENDENCE HALL) WHERE THE CONTINENTAL CONGRESS DEBATED THE COUNTRY'S MONEY PROBLEMS IN 1780.

THREE

Supplies

"We were absolutely, literally starved. I do solemnly declare that I did not put a single morsel of food into my mouth for four days."

Private Martin was describing conditions at Jockey Hollow in mid-January 1780.

The heavy, continuous snowstorms had sealed off the camp. Supply wagons simply could not get through.

Hunger—sickening, weakening, numbing hunger—stalked the soldiers constantly. Desperate, they stole food and livestock from local farms. Stealing had become an unfortunate necessity. Stories circulated of men gnawing on tree bark, cooking leather shoes, or eating horse food.

Dr. Thacher worried. "We are frequently for six or eight days entirely [without] meat, and then as long without bread. . . . The soldiers are so enfeebled from hunger and cold, as to be almost unable to perform their military duty, or labor in constructing their huts."

At the beginning of the war, the army promised each soldier a daily supply, or ration, of food that included bread, flour, meat or fish,

and peas or beans. In reality, a soldier hardly ever got that much food. Often the men received partial rations or none.

The army also had promised each soldier new clothing every year, including two pairs of shoes and a blanket. The soldiers didn't get those either; especially not two pairs of shoes and sometimes not even one pair. Half the troops were barefooted, leaving bloody footprints in the snow.

Private Martin said that he wore what could laughingly be called a uniform. And he possessed a blanket "thin enough to have straws shot through without discommoding the threads."

It was said that the men of the Pennsylvania Line wore what remained of the clothing they had when they'd enlisted nearly five years earlier. The average soldier had a patched coat, tattered shirt, worn pants, a one-third share of a blanket, and something to call shoes—or no shoes at all.

Brigadier General Anthony Wayne, in charge of the Pennsylvania Line, ranted about the lack of hats, shoes, and other clothing for his men. "They mean to leave us uniformly bare-headed—as well as bare-footed—and if they find that we can bare it tolerably well in the two extremes, perhaps they may try it in the center."

The lack of food and supplies was an enormous problem that lasted throughout the war.

When a supply wagon did plow through, the army had hardly any money for purchases.

The root of the supply problem was money. There was none.

The Continental Congress, a group of men chosen to govern the country, was in charge of the nation's money. The country didn't have a safe full of gold and silver. Congress didn't have laws permitting it to collect taxes. And unfortunately, wealthy nations were unwilling to loan money to the struggling new country. After all, if the Americans lost the war, they wouldn't be able to repay a loan. So Congress had no money and no way to get money.

The only thing Congress could do was print paper money, Continental dollars. The Continental Army bought supplies and paid the troops with Continental dollars. But this paper money was unsecured, meaning it wasn't backed up by gold and silver. When Congress ran out of money, it printed more. Then the states started printing their own paper money. Next, counterfeit or fake paper money showed up. As more and more paper money was printed, the value of a Continental dollar sank lower and lower. The country was drowning in paper money.

It took sixty Continental dollars to buy what one silver dollar could buy. The Continental dollar was worth so little that "not worth a Continental" became a lasting joke. Many local farmers wanted to sell their meat and vegetables to the Continental army. But they also wanted to sell their produce for good money. Sometimes their products ended up in the hands of the British, who could pay with gold and silver. The farmers didn't ask questions; they preferred not to know.

Washington was angry with the uncaring people who allowed the American army to continue to starve in the middle of rich farming country. He wrote many letters to Congress about the soldiers' suffering, lamenting that the army did not have the basic food supplies that were promised.

Washington told Congress, "The situation of the army, with respect to supplies, is beyond description, alarming. . . . We have never experienced a like extremity at any period of the war." He warned that unless Congress acted immediately, the soldiers would quit and go home for want of food. Privately, he worried that the hungry, weary soldiers would mutiny.

A committee of congressmen visited Jockey Hollow in 1780. They hoped to find that things were better than Washington had said. Instead they found that conditions were far worse. The army could barely feed the soldiers from one day to the next, some of the soldiers

COUNTERFEIT FORTY DOLLAR BILL. THE BRITISH ISSUE COUNTERFEIT PAPER MONEY TO ANNOY THE COLONISTS AND DISCREDIT CONGRESS. THE FAKES CONTRIBUTE TO THE DEPRECIATION OF THE CONTINENTAL DOLLAR.

hadn't been paid in five months, and the army had no money and no credit. At the time, each state enlisted, paid, and supplied its own regiments. The Massachusetts and Pennsylvania Lines hadn't been paid for a year. The committee told Congress that the soldiers faced hardships with courage and loyalty, but their patience was wearing thin. The daily hardships had produced a spirit of unrest among the troops. If the problems were not corrected, the entire cause would collapse. Still, Congress had no solution.

Have You Heard Grumbling about Money?

General de Kalb wrote to his family, "An ordinary horse is worth $20,000, I say twenty thousand dollars!" That was as much as he earned in ten years.

The good Doctor Thacher didn't waste words. He called paper money "trash."

One congressman said that paper money was only fit for making the tail of a kite.

Private Martin said, "I had 2 or 3 shillings of old Continental money, worth about as much as its weight in rags."

Washington ranted about the cost of "a rat in the shape of a horse."

And de Kalb wrote that the scarcity of clothing was unbelievable and grew from day to day. "A hat costs four hundred dollars, a pair of boots the same."

CONTINENTAL PAPER MONEY

FOR MORE about money explore www.kids.usa.gov. Select "money" and watch a video about how paper money is made or click "money games" and create your own "funny" paper money.

A winter soldier
plods on dispite his
bare toes.

FOUR

Manpower

"This was what has been termed the 'hard winter,' and hard it was to the poor soldiers."

That was Private Martin's opinion of the winter of 1779-80, his first winter at Jockey Hollow. No one there would have disagreed.

More than a thousand Continental soldiers deserted during the hard winter. One out of every ten gave up! They'd slip out of their huts in the middle of the night and duck into the Jockey Hollow woods before guards spotted them. They knew that if caught, they'd face severe punishment or possibly death. But they were desperate.

Lack of food, clothing, and money drove many to desert. Others left because they felt their families needed them more than the army did. Some deserters even joined the British to get warmer clothing and better pay.

General de Kalb believed that Jockey Hollow was no place for the average man. "An iron constitution like mine is required to bear up under this sort of usage," he said.

In addition to desertions, the army lost many soldiers because

BARON JOHANN DE KALB

their terms of service expired. Few chose to reenlist. The army was melting away.

New recruits were hard to find. In order to fill the ranks, the army offered new enlistees bonus money. This upset the long-suffering veterans because they had received much smaller bonuses. Now they were serving with new enlistees whose bonuses were ten times greater. Even though the bonuses were "not worth a Continental," the experienced veterans felt undervalued and overlooked.

"Our poor soldiers are reduced to the very verge of famine," Dr. Thacher said. "Their patience is exhausted by complicated sufferings, and their spirits are almost broken."

Broken spirits weren't limited to the privates. Officers, too, complained about the lack of food, clothing, and money. They were no longer able to support their families with worthless Continental paper money. Unlike the regular soldiers, officers could quit the army simply by resigning their commissions. Many resigned in disgust.

Washington tried to talk them into staying. But he found it hard when their reasons were problems at home or ill health. Washington allowed his trustworthy officers to spend the winter of 1779-80 at home with their families.

It was impossible to know the exact number

of soldiers at Jockey Hollow from one day to the next. But because of desertions and expired enlistments, Washington had only half the manpower he needed. He feared the British would learn of the shrinking army and attack. If they attacked, the much larger British army was sure to win.

The loyal soldiers who stayed at Jockey Hollow had their reasons for staying. Some had bonded with their fellow soldiers and felt they'd be letting their friends down by leaving. Others wanted the land that Congress promised to each soldier at the end of the war. Many firmly believed in the cause, America's right to be a free country.

As Private Martin put it, "We were unwilling to desert the cause of our country when in distress; we knew her cause involved our own."

On the other hand, good news from two sources did brighten spirits at Jockey Hollow in 1780.

First, the Marquis de Lafayette, a twenty-three-year-old French nobleman, brought a welcome announcement from the French government. Lafayette had joined the Continental Army in 1777 and had fought bravely at the battles of Brandywine and Monmouth. In 1779 he requested a leave of absence to return to France, hoping to persuade French officials to help the Americans. He returned in spring 1780. Lafayette arrived at Washington's Headquarters on May 10 to report France's promise of a loan, a superior fleet of ships, and thousands of troops to help fight the war. Washington was overjoyed by the extraordinary news, but worried that the army would dissolve before French aid arrived.

Lafayette himself remained in America and fought alongside the Americans through the end of the war. He became like a son to Washington.

The other good news was that the soldiers were much healthier at Jockey Hollow than in previous camps.

In 1776 hundreds of soldiers had died of smallpox, a disease that rapidly spread from one person to another. As a result Washington ordered smallpox inoculations for all soldiers.

About two thousand men had died at Valley Forge during the 1777-78 winter. Nine times more soldiers at Valley Forge had died of diseases than had died on the battlefields. Typhus fever and other diseases spread quickly in crowded army hospitals. Like the rest of the army, hospitals lacked supplies and the money to buy supplies.

Only eighty-six men died at Jockey Hollow during the hard winter.

The soldiers were healthier at Jockey Hollow because the huts were better built and better positioned on sloping hillsides for good drainage. In addition, the soldiers followed Army Surgeon James Tilton's rules for cleanliness, diet, and exercise. And they had hardened to the difficult life in camp.

Dr. Tilton, a well-known hospital planner at that time, looked at practices in American military hospitals. He saw soldiers brought into the hospital with battle wounds, but oftentimes carried out dead of typhus fever. So he designed a log-hut hospital that would limit the spread of diseases. Vents in the hospital walls and ceiling allowed fresh air to flow through the building. Wards—small rooms with no more than a dozen beds—separated patients with fevers from wounded soldiers.

The first hospital of this design was built in 1779-80 at Basking Ridge, New Jersey, near Morristown. Deaths from typhus dropped remarkably.

By mid-spring Dr. Thacher reported, "Our troops in camp are generally healthy, but we are troubled with . . . home sickness." He prescribed "a constant and active engagement of the mind."

But the doctor did not know that the starving, homesick soldiers soon would be in an "active engagement" with the enemy.

THE ARMY HOSPITAL AT BASKING RIDGE. FIREPLACE SMOKE ESCAPES THROUGH ROOF VENTS. THE HOSPITAL FLOOR PLAN SHOWS THREE SEPARATE WARDS: A CENTER WARD OF TWELVE BEDS FOR PATIENTS WITH CONTAGIOUS ILLNESSES AND TWO SIDE WARDS WITH EIGHT BEDS EACH FOR THE WOUNDED. THESE ILLUSTRATIONS ARE DERIVED FROM DR. TILTON'S ORIGINAL DRAWINGS.

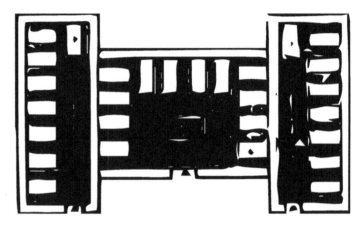

FOR MORE about the minutemen visit Minute Man National Historical Park at www.NPS.gov/mima. Click "Learn about the Park," select "Photos & Multimedia," then click "One Patriot Day in Concord" for a 25 minute video of events and activities on Patriots Day 2014 in Concord, Massachusetts.

Have You Heard about the Militiamen?

In colonial times, many men served as part-time soldiers in militias. They defended their towns and farms from raids, robberies, and other crimes. They also operated as lookouts and warned their neighbors of approaching enemies. In wartime, militias battled alongside the regular army when needed.

Militiamen, sometimes called Minutemen in the New England states, wore their regular clothes and used their own guns. Most used muskets, guns that fired accurately only over short distances. Woodsmen used Pennsylvania-made long rifles. Rifles fired five times farther than muskets and were more accurate, but took longer to load.

During the Revolution, armies fought head-to-head on flat, open battlefields using muskets and bayonets. Bayonets were pointed steel blades that attached to musket barrels.

Militias were more successful when they fought in a hit-and-run style. They would fire from behind barriers like trees, buildings, or fences. A militiaman would find a protected spot, fire at the enemy, run to a new spot, reload his gun, and fire again.

So while the two armies were battling head-to-head on an open battlefield, the British had the additional worry of militiamen firing at them from the woods. Even worse, they dreaded the hidden sharpshooters who were aiming their long rifles at them.

The three-pronged attack confused the British. It worked well for the Militiamen.

FIRING THE CANNON DURING A REENACTMENT OF THE BATTLE OF MONMOUTH IN 2014. REENACTMENTS ARE RECREATIONS OF HISTORIC EVENTS FOR PUBLIC ENTERTAINMENT AND EDUCATION.

FIVE

Battles

"The people are arming and training in every place. They are all liberty mad," wrote Nicholas Cresswell, a Briton visiting America in 1775. The war for liberty unfolded in a series of battles.

- In April **1775**, Minutemen battled the British Army at Lexington and Concord, Massachusetts. Someone fired the "shot heard 'round the world" and the armed revolt—now called the American Revolution—began.

- During **1776**, the Redcoats—the British soldiers—hammered the Continental Army at Long Island and drove them from New York, across New Jersey, and into Pennsylvania. Britain thought the war was over. But the Continentals roared back. Washington and his men crossed the Delaware River at

In colonial America, citizens who wanted the country to be a free and independent nation were called Patriots or Rebels. Those who wanted the country to remain a British colony and remained loyal to the king were known as Loyalists. The British soldiers were dubbed Redcoats because they wore red jackets.

night, surprised the enemy, and took back Trenton and Princeton, New Jersey.

• The British won the battle at Brandywine, Pennsylvania in September **1777**, then moved their headquarters to Philadelphia. The next month the Americans won a major battle at Saratoga, New York and captured seven thousand enemy soldiers.

• In the summer of **1778**, Washington led the army and militias in an attack on the Redcoats at Monmouth Courthouse in New Jersey. The British lost two thousand troops at Monmouth. They packed up during the night and escaped to New York, their new headquarters. Upset with events in the North, Britain sent troops to the South. They took control of Savannah, Georgia and held it for four years.

• The Continental army attacked two enemy-held forts in **1779**. Brigadier General Anthony Wayne and his men captured the fort at Stoney Point, New York during a midnight raid. They boldly waded through marshlands and scaled cliffs overhanging the Hudson River to take the fort and destroy its ammunition. They captured five hundred prisoners. Wayne suffered a severe head wound, yet his men helped the gritty general stagger into the fort to celebrate. Wayne reported, "Our officers and men behaved like men who are determined to be free." A month later Major Harry Lee took the fort at Paulus Hook, New Jersey. These two important victories stopped enemy shipping on the Hudson River north of Stoney Point. Congress awarded both Wayne and Lee gold medals. The victories stirred the American Patriots' pride and spirits.

When the starved and ragged Continentals marched to Jockey Hollow for the hard winter of 1779-80, they'd been fighting the most powerful country in the world for five years. However, neither army was winning the war.

During the hard winter, the British raided homes around Elizabethtown, New Jersey, across the Hudson River from their camp. When they could trudge through the snow, they broke into homes, stole or destroyed possessions, took prisoners, and burned buildings. Residents despised the Redcoats. American soldiers and militias harassed the raiders at every opportunity.

In May the worst possible news arrived from the South. The Continental Army in South Carolina had lost Charleston to the British. The Redcoats had come ashore out of the range of Fort Moultrie's powerful cannons. They surrounded the outnumbered Americans and closed off all paths of retreat. Their cannons pounded the trapped soldiers until they surrendered. The British took the entire force of five thousand Americans as prisoners. Losing Charleston was the Continental Army's largest loss of manpower and equipment

during the war. Britain believed the South was theirs.

Washington sent Major General de Kalb and two thousand soldiers from Jockey Hollow to help the depleted American force in the South.

Meanwhile, new trouble erupted in the North. Washington's spies near Elizabethtown reported that the enemy was marching into New Jersey. Five thousand British soldiers invaded New Jersey on June 7, 1780. They planned to march to Morristown, blow up military supplies, defeat the army at Jockey Hollow, and end the war in the North. The invaders set out toward Hobart Gap, a pass through the Watchung Mountains. They would march through the two small New Jersey villages of Connecticut Farms (now Union, New Jersey) and Springfield.

As the men at Jockey Hollow prepared for battle, the warning cannon called "Old Sow" boomed and signal beacons blazed on the Watchung Mountain ridges to alert the residents and militias. Reverend James Caldwell, a minister, a soldier, and a local "Paul Revere," raced through the countryside to rally the militiamen. Loyalists hated Reverend Caldwell for his rebellious sermons. They called him the "Rebel High Priest."

BATTLE OF FORT MOULTRIE, CHARLESTON, SOUTH CAROLINA, 1776. A SOLDIER REPLACES THE FLAG DURING A BRITISH ATTACK. THE BRITISH RETREAT BUT RETURN IN 1780, SAILING OUTSIDE THE RANGE OF THE FORT'S CANNONS AND CAPTURING CHARLESTON. THESE CANNONS ARE REPRODUCTIONS OF THE 18-POUNDERS AT FORT MOULTRIE IN 1776.

Patriot militiamen respected him and responded to the call. They wanted the British to pay for ruthlessly raiding their villages.

Militiamen hid along the enemy's route. As the Redcoats marched by, the Rebels surprised them by shooting from behind fences and hedges, from woods and orchards, and from inside buildings. If driven off, the militiamen turned up farther down the road and continued firing.

For most of the day the Jockey Hollow soldiers held their own on the battlefield at Connecticut Farms. British troops greatly outnumbered the Continentals, but the

Americans firmly resisted. They continued to fire at the enemy while they were being pushed back.

Eventually the Americans were pushed out of Connecticut Farms. The Redcoats looted homes in the village and then set it on fire. Someone shot through the window of the minister's house and killed his wife, Hannah Caldwell, while she sat with her small children. This horrifically cruel and pointless act enraged the Americans.

In the evening the British retired to high ground. "Liberty-mad" militiamen peppered shots at them until dark. After dark the invaders quietly slipped back to Elizabethtown to wait for reinforcements.

Two weeks later spies spotted a fleet of British ships sailing toward the Hudson River, possibly to attack West Point, New York. Washington personally led the main army from Jockey Hollow toward West Point to boost its defenses. The fort at West Point was valuable because it controlled all Hudson River traffic from New York to New England and Canada. However, the British fleet stopped well south of West Point, unloaded gear, and set up camp. The Redcoats pitched tents, foraged for hay for their horses, and relaxed in the fields. Later they reloaded their ships and sailed back to headquarters in New York. Washington and his men were relieved but baffled.

Meanwhile, General Nathanael Greene took over as commander of the greatly reduced force at Jockey Hollow, now only 1,500 men.

On June 23, spies informed Greene that the British were on the move toward Morristown. This time six thousand Redcoats marched out of Elizabethtown. Again, booming blasts from "Old Sow" and smoky flames from the signal beacons rallied the militias. Militiamen hurried to hiding spots along Vauxhall and Galloping Hill Roads. They were ready to harass the invaders when they passed.

At Jockey Hollow Dr. Thacher reported, "At 6 o'clock in the morning of the 23d, the alarm guns were fired. The drums throughout

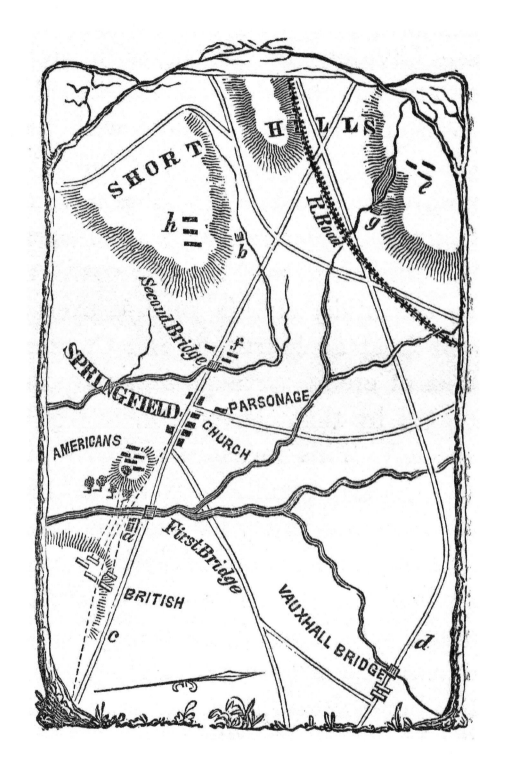

our camp beat to arms, announcing the approach of the enemy; the whole army is instantly in motion." He said that the soldiers looked composed, yet excited and steeled for defense. "Soon after the alarm, our advance party, consisting of General Maxwell's brigade and a few militias, discovered the enemy advancing toward the village of Springfield."

Greene ordered the Rhode Island regiment to defend the Springfield bridge.

"Colonel Israel Angell's regiment of Rhode Island . . . were posted at a bridge over which the enemy were to pass," Dr. Thacher said. "Their [Britain's] whole force, of five or six thousand men, was actually held in check by these brave soldiers for more than forty minutes." Thacher was on the battlefield the entire day tending the wounded.

During the battle the Continentals called for more wadding—paper to shove down their musket barrels to hold the shot in place. According to legend, Reverend Caldwell heard the call. He raced to the church and returned with hymnals of songs written by Isaac Watts. Reverend Caldwell ripped out clumps of pages and tossed them to the soldiers, shouting, "Put Watts in 'em, boys!" That afternoon "Give 'em Watts" became the American rallying cry.

Throughout the battle the Americans were slowly pushed out of Springfield, toward the mountainsides around Hobart Gap. They regrouped on the slopes and prepared to defend the pass through the Watchung Mountains.

With the Americans out of Springfield, the British set fire to that town too. They spared four loyalists' homes. Everything else was

BATTLE OF SPRINGFIELD, JUNE 23, 1780.
MAP LEGEND – *a*: CONNECTICUT FARMS, *b* & *g*: CANNONS,
c: GALLOPING HILL ROAD, *d*: VAUXHALL ROAD,
e & *h*: AMERICANS ON HILLSIDES, *R.Road*: RAILROAD DID NOT EXIST IN 1780.

burned. One soldier said that they even torched the pig sties. While Springfield blazed the invaders settled down for a long lunch.

General Greene rushed a message to Washington. "They [the British] are directing their force against this pass [Hobart Gap], which I am determined to dispute so far as I am capable."

When the British resumed their march down Galloping Hill and Vauxhall, the scene before them stopped them in their tracks. The steep slopes at Hobart Gap were dotted with Continentals, waiting for them. Militiamen swarmed over the slopes of Newark Mountain, ready to take aim. When the Redcoats moved forward, cannon blasts and gunfire from both sides greeted them. The small but resilient American army knew its way around the mountains. They had set up a fearsome defense. The British quickly decided to quit rather than push through the heavily guarded Gap.

As the Redcoats rapidly retreated to New York, furious militiamen stormed after them, pelting them every step of the way. They'd gone "liberty-mad" again. And why not? Some had just watched their homes burn to the ground.

Eyewitness Thacher reported, "Our troops were commanded by Major General Greene; not more than one thousand were brought into action at any one time. Their conduct was marked with the commendable coolness and [fearlessness] of veteran troops."

The British never launched another major invasion in the North. Instead they shifted the fighting to the South. Morristown's ammunition supplies remained safe. And the Jockey Hollow army survived.

The American camp didn't understand why the enemy had retreated at Springfield.

Perhaps the British knew they'd never overcome the residents' growing hatred of them, the militias' endless sniping at them, and the soldiers' perseverance against all odds. Or maybe they were simply looking for an easier way to win the war.

No one in the American camp would have predicted the storm that was about to erupt.

Have You Heard about Reenactors and Living Historians?

Historic reenactments recreate significant events from history for the purpose of entertaining and educating the public. For example, the Friends of Monmouth Battlefield schedule an annual reenactment of the Battle of Monmouth in New Jersey. Reenactors dress, eat, and speak like colonial Americans for the duration of the event, but live modern lifestyles with careers outside of reenacting.

Living historians are professional interpreters or tradespeople who are employed by historical museums like Colonial Williamsburg in Virginia. They have a comprehensive knowledge of their field enabling them to create an in-depth representation of the past as part of their job.

REENACTORS' TENT AT COWPENS NATIONAL BATTLEFIELD IN 2015

WASHINGTON CROSSING THE DELAWARE REENACTMENT IN 2009

FOR MORE about Washington's crossing, go to the Mount Vernon website at www.mountvernon.org. Search for "The Winter Patriots" and watch a not-to-be-missed series of videos covering Washington crossing the Delaware and battling at Trenton and Princeton.

BRITISH SPY JOHN ANDRÉ (LEFT) MEETS BENEDICT ARNOLD (RIGHT)
AT WEST POINT, NEW YORK.

SIX

Treason

Before dawn on September 26, 1780, fifes and drums called the soldiers to assemble for an alarming announcement from Major General Nathanael Greene.

"Treason of the blackest dye was yesterday discovered! General Arnold, who commanded at West Point . . . , was about to deliver up that important Post into the hands of the enemy. Such an event [would] have given the American cause a deadly wound if not fatal stab. Happily the treason has been timely discovered to prevent the fatal misfortune."

Private Martin probably spoke for all the soldiers when he said, "It was reported that General Arnold had deserted. I should as soon have thought West Point had deserted as he, but I was soon convinced that it was true."

Benedict Arnold was born in America to a well-to-do family in Connecticut. Due to his father's poor health, however, the Arnolds lost all their money by the time Benedict was fourteen. His mother died when he was eighteen, and his father died two years later.

Arnold captained a Connecticut militia unit when the fight for freedom erupted in 1775. He and Ethan Allen commanded militias at the battle of Fort Ticonderoga in New York State. They won the battle and brought back seventy-eight cannons, thousands of cannonballs, and other much-needed weapons. Later that year Arnold fought in the American army's failed attempt to capture Quebec Province, Canada. Congress had hoped to convince Quebec residents to join the American Revolution. Arnold was shot in the foot during fierce combat.

Washington respected and valued Arnold. He trusted him completely.

In 1775 Washington wrote, "The merit of this gentleman [Arnold] is certainly great and I heartily wish that fortune may distinguish him as one of her favorites. . . . I am convinced that he will do everything that prudence and valor shall suggest, to add to the success of [the war]."

Two years later a fully recovered Arnold fought with courage and spirit in the Battle of Saratoga. He fearlessly rode his horse among the fighting soldiers and shouted encouragement. The Redcoats shot his horse out from under him, and Arnold suffered another leg wound that led to a painful, incurable limp.

Arnold's heroics, bravery, and wounds were real. And yet Congress passed over him when they appointed five new major generals. He felt slighted and mistreated because he had served the army longer than any of the appointees had served. Moreover, he'd been wounded twice, one a permanent injury.

When the British left Philadelphia in 1778, Washington put Arnold in charge of that city. Benedict and his wife, Peggy Shippen Arnold, set up a fine household and spent money carelessly. Their debts mounted.

ARNOLD CONTINUES FIRING HIS PISTOL AT THE BRITISH WHILE PINNED UNDER HIS FALLEN HORSE DURING THE BATTLE OF SARATOGA.

Upset with the treatment he received from the Continental Army and unable to pay his bills, Arnold grew desperate. Peggy introduced her husband to British Major John André, a friend of hers. André was in charge of Britain's spying activities.

Arnold met with André to propose a deal. Arnold offered to hand over West Point to Britain. In return he asked for twenty thousand pounds in gold and silver and, because he felt overlooked by his own country, a position in the British army. The enemy was interested. If the British controlled West Point and the Hudson River, they could block the connection between the Northern states and the rest of America. They would cut the country in two and end the war.

Arnold asked Washington to appoint him commander of West Point. He used his limp as an excuse to request a less active post. Washington agreed in an attempt to satisfy the moody officer.

As commander of West Point, Arnold began weakening its defenses and using up its supplies so the British could more easily capture the fort. To complete the betrayal, Arnold met with André at West Point. Arnold gave the British spy detailed plans for turning over the fort. André tucked the plans into his boot for safekeeping.

During André's trip back to New York, three American militiamen stopped him. They questioned him and searched him. The militiamen found the papers in his boot and thought the documents looked important. So they sent the papers to headquarters.

Washington was stunned. He had valued and trusted Arnold, yet Arnold had betrayed him. If Arnold could betray him, who could he trust? The general worried that all his officers, as well as the soldiers, had reached the breaking point.

The timing of events leading to the discovery of Arnold's treachery was uncannily lucky. British ships had already been loaded for the attack on West Point.

After Arnold learned that André had been captured, he fled to a British ship that waited just outside the range of West Point's cannons. Arnold escaped, leaving West Point undefended!

Brigadier General Wayne and his Pennsylvanians were stationed at Haverstraw, New York when he learned of the defection. In the middle of the night, they marched sixteen miles over mountains in four hours to defend West Point. On their arrival Washington was relieved and said that all was safe again.

Meanwhile at Tappan, New York, Major André stood trial. He was

well educated, artistic, honorable, and like-
able. But his crime was grave. Losing West
Point could have lost the war for the Americans. André was tried, found guilty, and
hanged as a spy. Before he was hanged, he
bowed to his captors and serenely accepted
his fate. André died bravely.

Arnold, on the other hand, joined the enemy. He fought the remainder of the war as
an officer in the British army. After the war

MILITIAMEN DISCOVER
DOCUMENTS IN ANDRÉ'S
BOOT.

he and Peggy lived the rest of their lives in Britain.

Dr. Thacher correctly predicted, "The pages of our history will be tarnished by the record of crimes . . . by a native of our land."

One officer described the crime as a dark hour for the American cause.

Darker hours loomed.

FOR MORE about the Great Chain, check out Lincoln Diamant's book, Chaining the Hudson, the Fight for the River in the American Revolution. *(New York: Carol Publishing Group, 1994)*

Have You Heard about Washington's Watch Chain?

The fort at West Point controlled traffic on the Hudson River. Washington knew the British wanted the fort, so he strengthened its defenses in 1778.

He had a sixty-five-ton iron chain constructed and installed across the Hudson. The Great Chain stretched from West Point to Constitution Island. Each of its eight hundred links was two feet long and weighed a hundred and twenty-five pounds. Heavy log rafts with anchors kept the chain afloat and held it in place. Washington's engineers believed it would block all enemy shipping on the Hudson.

Soldiers installed the chain in April 1778. To avoid ice damage, they removed the chain every fall and reinstalled it in spring. The process involved many men and took several days. The troops dubbed it "Washington's Watch Chain."

The soldiers drew up the chain for the last time when the war ended. West Point kept thirteen links of the Great Chain, one for each original state. The remaining links were recycled.

Oddly, the British never tested the chain. So even though the chain never physically stopped an enemy ship, its mere presence did.

THIRTEEN WROUGHT IRON LINKS FROM THE GREAT CHAIN SURROUND A BRITISH CANNON TAKEN AT STONEY POINT AND TWO SMALLER CANNONS CAPTURED AT SARATOGA. ALL ARE PRESERVED AT WEST POINT MUSEUM.

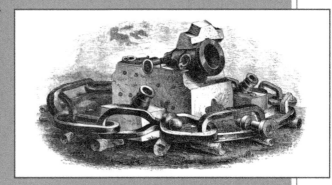

F C YOHN

SEVEN

Mutiny

Two years before the men arrived at Jockey Hollow, General Washington had praised the loyalty and patience of the starving, freezing, ragged soldiers at Valley Forge and admitted relief that they had not been driven "by their sufferings, to a general mutiny or dispersion."

The Commander-in-Chief feared mutiny more than any other crime the men might commit. Mutiny could infect the whole army and crush all hope for independence. Washington repeatedly wrote Congress about the ongoing lack of food, clothing, and pay. With no money and little power, Congress was unable to help. The soldiers grew more restless.

In January 1780, Dr. Thacher reported, "About two hundred soldiers of the Massachusetts Line who were stationed at West Point, pretending that their term of enlistment had expired, marched off with the intention of going home. . . . Troops were dispatched after them, and they were brought back." Thacher said that those whose terms had expired were discharged. But he added, "Many of them had several months to serve: some of these were punished, and the remainder returned to their duty."

Five months later two Connecticut regiments at Jockey Hollow threatened to desert in search of food. The angry, starving men burst from their huts with loaded weapons and declared they would confront local farmers with bayonets to obtain food. Private Martin's regiment was one of the threatening units. He described the disgruntled men as "growling like soreheaded dogs."

Martin explained, "They saw no other alternative but to starve to death, or break up the army . . . . To give up all was too much, but to starve to death was too much also. Here was . . . their country sitting still and expecting the army to do notable things while fainting from sheer starvation."

Colonel Walter Stewart reminded the men that they had won immortal honor by their perseverance and bravery; but now they were throwing all that away. The snarling men calmed down and returned to their huts. Frustration persisted.

Washington wrote to Congress about the Connecticut uprising. "This matter . . . has given me infinitely more concern than anything that has ever happened." He warned that mutiny would continue to be a threat until Congress resolved the clothing, food, and pay problems. The Connecticut men had not been paid for five months. Later the weary commander admitted, "Indeed, I have almost ceased to hope."

By far the largest and most dangerous revolt erupted during the second winter camp at Jockey Hollow in 1780-81. Two thousand soldiers of the Pennsylvania Line were the only troops camped at Jockey Hollow that winter. Brigadier General Anthony Wayne was in command. Wayne warned Joseph Reed, head of the Pennsylvania Council, that the state had neglected and ignored its soldiers for too long.

"INDEED, I HAVE ALMOST CEASED TO HOPE," WASHINGTON WROTE IN 1780.

Wayne told Reed, "They [the Pennsylvania Line] have now served their country for near five years, poorly clothed, badly fed, and worse paid . . . they have not seen a paper dollar in the way of pay for near twelve months . . . . Believe me, my dear sir, that if something is not done to give them a local attachment to this country and to quiet their minds, we have not yet seen the worst side of the picture."

On New Year's Day 1781, the desperate Pennsylvania Line gathered with guns and backpacks. They took cannons, ammunition, muskets, tents, and horses. They were determined to march to

Philadelphia and present their grievances to the Continental Congress and the Pennsylvania Council.

They shared the same complaints as all the other soldiers: lack of food and warm clothing; no pay. But the Pennsylvanians had an even greater problem that was uniquely theirs. They disputed their terms of enlistment. Pennsylvanians enlisted for three years or the duration of the war. While other states released their troops after three years, Pennsylvania did not. The Pennsylvania Council insisted that "duration of the war" was the binding rule.

The soldiers believed they should have been discharged months, even years, earlier. They wanted what they'd been promised. They said they had no intention of deserting. They said they were not "Arnolds."

In spite of their sufferings, the Pennsylvanians were among the best soldiers in the army. Historians say they were the backbone of the army, experienced, brave, and bold. They served from 1775 to the victory at Yorktown in 1781 and fought in almost every major battle. Many had joined Wayne in the daring victory at Stoney Point. And they were the dependable soldiers who had rushed to West Point in the middle of the night after Arnold left the fort undefended.

Wayne tried to calm them, but they refused to listen. The officers tried to restrain them, but a scuffle broke out. In the confusion an officer and a soldier were killed; others were wounded.

When Wayne aimed his pistols at the group, a fence of bayonets surrounded him. One man shouted, "We love you, we respect you, but you are a dead man if you fire. Do not mistake us; we are not going to the enemy." He added that, if the British were to attack right now, they would fight under Wayne's orders with "as much resolution and eagerness as ever."

The officers were overwhelmingly outnumbered and had no choice but to let the men go.

The Pennsylvania soldiers began their march to Philadelphia in orderly columns. No one attempted to escape to the British. They didn't steal food from the farms they passed. The public supported them and called them "the honest mutineers."

One eyewitness said that they marched so precisely that it looked like they were "under military discipline."

Wayne, Colonel Walter Stewart, and Colonel Richard Butler followed.

The mutineers had elected a Board of Sergeants to speak for them. The Board insisted

MUTINY: ANTHONY WAYNE, 1781
COLORED ENGRAVING, NINETEENTH CENTURY.

on speaking directly to the Pennsylvania Council. Joseph Reed, president of the Pennsylvania Council, agreed to meet with the sergeants at Princeton, New Jersey. The sergeants stayed in Nassau Hall at Princeton. The men camped in tents nearby.

Meanwhile at West Point, Washington wrote to all state governors, "It is in vain to think an army can be kept together much longer under such a variety of sufferings as ours has experienced." He warned that unless the soldiers received at least three months' pay, ample food, and warm clothing immediately, the entire army would dissolve.

NEW JERSEY COLLEGE IN PRINCETON, 1850 (NOW KNOWN AS NASSAU HALL AT PRINCETON UNIVERSITY)

Back at Princeton, the Board of Sergeants spelled out their long-standing grievances to Reed. Reed listened carefully and proposed settlement terms. Soldiers who had completed their three-year enlistments would be discharged. Back pay, with adjustments for the falling value of paper money, would be made as soon as possible. He told the men that the Council had already purchased new clothing that would arrive at Trenton in a few days. He upheld Wayne's promise to pardon the mutineers.

The majority of the mutineers agreed to the terms. So nine days after the uprising, the soldiers marched in strict military form to Trenton for supplies. Each received a pair of shoes, overalls, a shirt, and a blanket. Each got a month's pay and a sixty-day leave of absence. More than one thousand Pennsylvanians remained in service and many of the discharged men reenlisted.

Wayne told Washington, "I hope [in] a few weeks . . . to announce to your Excellency a reclaimed and formidable Line. . . . The storm has subsided."

Dr. Thacher called the mutiny "a most unfortunate transaction, which might have been prevented, had the just complaints of the army received proper attention." Many agreed.

The storm had not completely subsided, however. Within weeks of the Pennsylvania mutiny, three hundred New Jersey soldiers left their posts at Pompton, New Jersey. They cited their need for food, clothing, and shelter. Some suffered from frostbite and other illnesses. None had been paid for months. They didn't intend to desert or join the British; they just wanted the same terms that the Pennsylvanians had gotten. Although New Jersey had already decided to extend some of the Pennsylvanians' benefits to the New Jersey Line, unfortunately the soldiers had not yet been told.

An alarmed General Washington wanted to enforce severe

punishments to stop further outbreaks. His orders to Major General Robert Howe were clear. "If you succeed in compelling the revolted troops to surrender, you will instantly execute a few of the most active and [troublesome] leaders."

Howe directed armed New England troops to surround the unarmed mutineers. On the spot, Howe tried the ringleaders. He found two men guilty. He ordered them shot to death by their fellow soldiers, in front of all the troops.

This was the soldiers' darkest hour.

FOR MORE about Jockey Hollow, visit Morristown National Historical Park's website at www.nps.gov/morr. Click "Learn about the Park" and explore the choices.

Have You Heard about the 265-Year-Old Wick House?

Henry Wick, his wife Mary, and their twenty-one-year-old daughter Temperance, called Tempe, were Patriots who clearly supported the Revolutionary War. They allowed Washington's Army to camp on their Jockey Hollow farm. They permitted the army to cut down six hundred acres of trees to build huts and to use as firewood. Henry Wick himself volunteered with the Morris County Cavalry. In addition the Wicks shared their home with Major General Arthur St. Clair.

The Wicks built this house around 1750. It still stands in near-original condition, and at its original location. Today the house, as well as most of the Wick farm, is part of Morristown National Historical Park. Gardens, orchards, fields, and a barnyard surround the 265-year-old house. The house is open to the public as an example of a colonial farmhouse.

The house is the subject of an old myth. According to the tale, when the mutiny erupted Tempe hid her horse in a back bedroom in-side the Wick house. She feared that the mutineers would steal her horse for their trip to Philadelphia. When the mutineers arrived at the farm, they didn't think of searching the house. Tempe's horse was saved. The story has been retold for generations, even though no evidence has ever been found to prove it happened.

EIGHT

Perseverance

"Huzza for the Americans!" shouted the French soldiers at Yorktown, Virginia in 1781. "Huzza" was a colonial expression of joy, like hooray.

Britain had shifted the war to the South after its defeat at Springfield, New Jersey. But the Americans in the South were earning huzzas while the North was dealing with treason and mutinies.

Continentals and militias had lost a major battle at Camden, South Carolina in August 1780. Commander Horatio Gates panicked under furious cannon fire and fled the battlefield. He didn't stop until he was sixty miles away. When Washington learned of the desertion, he chose General Nathanael Greene to replace Gates as commander of the Southern Army.

GENERAL WASHINGTON AND FRENCH GENERAL ROCHAMBEAU OVERSEE THE BATTLE OF YORKTOWN

After Greene arrived in the South, he divided the troops into small units. He planned to use them to spring surprise attacks on enemy outposts. Greene didn't have enough men to defeat the British in a major battle, so he hoped to wear the Redcoats down by harassing them at every opportunity.

General Francis Marion and his men attacked enemy supply lines. The British called him "Swamp Fox" because he led his men through the South Carolina swamps to escape capture.

Patriot militias defeated Loyalists militias at King's Mountain, South Carolina in October 1780. Most were mountain men, hunters and woodsmen from the Carolinas and Virginia. They typically wore fringed hunting shirts and carried long rifles. It was a bitter battle of neighbor

MOUNTAIN MAN HIDDEN IN A FOREST. BY GERRY EMBLETON

against neighbor, but the Patriots' victory boosted their spirits and determination.

In January 1781, General Daniel Morgan led Continentals and woodsmen militias into battle at Cowpens, South Carolina. The spot was called Cowpens because frontier settlers brought their cattle there to graze. Morgan designed a battle plan that took advantage of his men's skills and is still considered a masterpiece. In less than an hour, the British defense collapsed. Morgan reported to General Greene that his men obtained a complete victory over the British troops commanded by Lieutenant Colonel Tarleton. But to his friends, Morgan proudly announced that he had given Tarleton and the Redcoats "a devil of a whipping."

Two months later Greene and his men fought the British at Guilford Courthouse in North Carolina. The British commander, General Cornwallis, claimed victory; but he lost many more soldiers than the Americans lost. To reinforce Greene's army, Washington sent Lafayette and twelve hundred men south. They trailed Cornwallis's army, harassed them, and engaged them in skirmishes and firefights.

By August, Cornwallis needed fresh troops and supplies. He had lost thousands of soldiers in battles and skirmishes over the past ten months. The survivors were exhausted; many were sick or wounded. The British commander led his weary troops to Yorktown, Virginia on the York River near Chesapeake Bay. There they could rest while waiting for ships to bring aid from New York. Lafayette learned of Cornwallis's plan and rushed news of the enemy's location to Washington.

At the same time, Washington learned that French ships and troops—the help that Lafayette had promised when he arrived in Morristown sixteen months before—were finally on the way. The fleet was sailing from the French West Indies to Chesapeake Bay. So

Have You Heard of Morgan's Masterpiece?

Brigadier General Daniel Morgan knew that the British regulars and cavalry outnumbered his force at the Battle of Cowpens. Although his troops were experienced and courageous, the British were better tacticians. The Americans' strength was its skill with rifles—guns that could shoot farther and more accurately than British muskets.

Morgan's plan took advantage of his soldiers' skills. He chose a battlefield with three low mounds that were separated by wide depressions. He positioned his sharpshooting riflemen at the first mound. They would slow down the enemy's advance and then fall back. Militias assembled at the second mound with orders to fire two volleys when the Redcoats were at a "killing distance," then fall behind the Continentals who lined up on the third mound. Morgan placed the cavalry behind the Continentals, ready to fight.

When the advancing British Army saw the front line of American riflemen, Tarleton ordered a cavalry charge to drive them back. As the regular British soldiers came within range, the militia fired, aiming for the British officers. The militiamen then withdrew behind the third line. In the confusion, the Continentals misunderstood an order and the entire line began to retreat. Morgan quickly reassembled the line. They stood their ground and fired point-blank at the advancing Redcoats. The American cavalry joined the fight and British resistance crumbled.

In the end the Redcoats suffered four times more losses than the Americans. Morgan's tactical masterpiece inspired the public in all thirteen colonies.

while the enemy's exhausted troops were recovering in Yorktown, French warships were sailing straight toward them.

Washington realized all his forces would be needed in the South. He assembled his Northern army, including the Jockey Hollow regiments, and began marching to Yorktown in mid-August. Militias joined them along the way. While the foot soldiers marched, twenty-nine French warships carrying three thousand ground troops sailed into Chesapeake Bay. Huzza for the French!

By the time Washington's army reached Yorktown in mid-September, the French fleet already had driven the British navy out of

BATTLE OF THE VIRGINIA CAPES. FRENCH SHIPS (LEFT) BATTLE BRITISH SHIPS (RIGHT) IN SEPTEMBER, 1781.

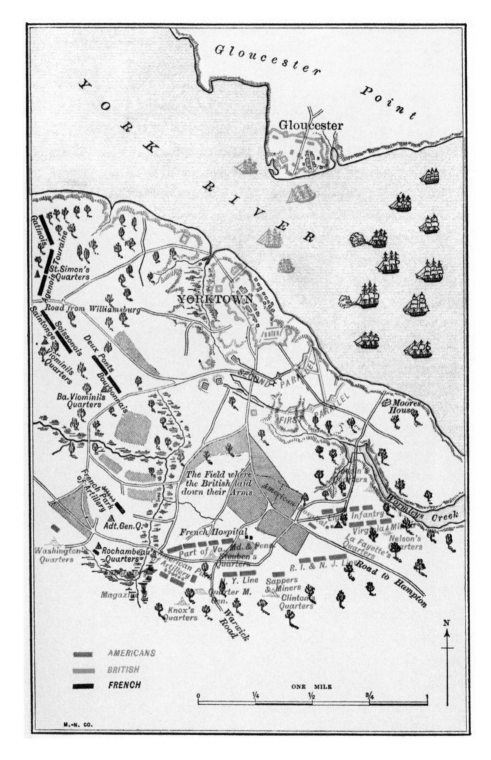

Map of Yorktown and Gloucester. Labels visible on the map include:

Gloucester Point

Gloucester

YORK RIVER

Rochenois
St. Simon's Quarters
Touraine
Road from Williamsburg
Saintonge
Soissonois
Deux Ponts
Bourbonnais
Ba. Viominil's Quarters
Viominil's Quarters

YORKTOWN

SECOND PARALLEL
FIRST PARALLEL
Moores House

French Park of Artillery

The Field where the British laid down their Arms

Wormleys Creek

Adt. Gen. Q.

French Hospital

Washington Quarters
Rochambeau's Quarters
Part of American Park of Artillery
Part of Va. Md. & Penn. Steuben's Quarters

Light Infantry
Virginia Milita
Nelson's Quarters
La Fayette's Quarters
R. I. & N. J. Line
Road to Hampton

Magazine
Y. Line
Quarter M. Gen.
Sappers & Miners
Clinton Quarters

Knox's Quarters
Warwick Road

N

AMERICANS
BRITISH
FRENCH

ONE MILE
0   ¼   ½   ¾

M.-N. CO.

the bay and back to New York. It was the first time the French navy had defeated the British navy in a century. Now the French controlled Chesapeake Bay, and Cornwallis's much-needed troops and supplies would not get through.

The combined French-American allies (partners) began digging trenches and setting up cannons for battle. This time the allies had more troops and cannons than the British had, inspiring the high-spirited General Wayne to predict a glorious victory for the American cause.

Martin, now promoted to sergeant, was on the Yorktown battlefield. On October 9, 1781, he reported that everyone was on "the tip toe of expectation" and ready for the battle to begin. Raising the American flag would be the signal to begin firing.

"About noon, the much-wished-for signal went up," Sergeant Martin wrote. "I confess I felt a secret pride swell my heart when I saw the 'star-spangled banner' waving majestically in the very faces of our [enemies]. . . . A simultaneous discharge of all the guns in the line followed, the French troops accompanying it with 'Huzza for the Americans!'"

Dr. Thacher was also at Yorktown and noted, "General Washington put the match

BATTLE OF YORKTOWN, OCTOBER 15 - 19, 1781.

to the first gun, and a furious discharge of cannon and mortars immediately followed."

The allied armies quickly surrounded the Redcoats. More than one hundred cannons pounded the trapped enemy.

Thacher described the battle. "From the 10th to the 15th [of October], a tremendous and [nonstop] firing from the American and French batteries is kept up. . . . All around was thunder and lightning from our numerous cannon and mortars, and in the darkness of night, presents one of the most sublime and magnificent spectacles which can be imagined. Some of our shells . . . fall into the river, and bursting, throw up columns of water like the spouting of the monsters of the deep."

The attack destroyed British defenses. Cornwallis was running out of ammunition. Many of his men were wounded. All were hungry. With no hope for supplies and fresh troops to arrive, there was no choice. Cornwallis surrendered.

Both sides agreed to terms, and a formal surrender occurred on October 19. That day, the American troops proudly and joyously lined one side of the road to Yorktown. The French soldiers lined the other side, looking pleased and polished in blue and white uniforms. The two columns of victorious soldiers stretched for more than a mile.

Dr. Thacher, on horseback, had a good view of the event. He reported that Cornwallis did not attend, pleading illness. General O'Hara led the British soldiers in a "slow and solemn" march between the lines of American and French soldiers. American General Benjamin Lincoln directed the defeated army to a field where they were to lay down their arms. According to Thacher, they laid down their arms in a "very unofficer like manner . . . throwing their arms on the pile with

John Trumbull Yorktown Flag, one of several flags carried by the Continentals during the Revolution. The Americans are flying this flag in Trumbull's painting.

violence." They had just lost a major battle and were about to become prisoners of war.

On the other hand, the Americans were excited and overjoyed. One official said, "The officers and soldiers could scarcely talk for laughing, and they could scarcely walk for jumping and dancing and singing as they went about."

Yorktown was a decisive victory for America. England began talks to end the war.

After Yorktown, Washington sent most of his troops back north. The main army camped near West Point during the 1781-82 winter. However, the New Jersey Brigade returned to Jockey Hollow to keep an eye on the British in New York City. More than two hundred raids and skirmishes occurred in New Jersey after the Battle of Springfield and before the official end of the war.

New Jersey troops, the last to occupy Jockey Hollow, left their log-house city in August 1782. Washington ordered them closer to the British. Thus Jockey Hollow—with its rugged hills that had sheltered the weary soldiers from the enemy—ended its history as a military camp.

But the fighting wasn't over. The British refused to leave Charleston and Savannah without a battle. Commander Greene and Brigadier General Wayne with the brave Pennsylvanians fought the final chapter of the war. They battled Redcoats, Loyalist militias, and Native American tribes around Savannah beginning in January 1782. The British were forced from Savannah in July. The Americans reclaimed Charleston in December.

John Adams, an American statesman and future president, was drafting the peace treaty at the time. He saw the importance of reclaiming Charleston and Savannah. He said that Greene's last action in the South was as important for America as the surrender of

Cornwallis; the result was a complete victory. If America had not reclaimed those cities, the Deep South would have remained in British hands.

British and American officials signed the Treaty of Paris on September 3, 1783. Finally, the war officially ended. America was now a free nation. Huzza for the Americans!

Years later, Joseph Martin remembered the day he was discharged. "There was as much sorrow as joy," he wrote. "We had lived together as a family of brothers for several years . . . and now we were to be . . . parted forever."

James Thacher shared those feelings,

saying that his wartime friendships were as binding as "the ties of brotherly affection."

George Washington, too, described his Army as "one patriotic band of Brothers" in his farewell to the troops.

At New York harbor, Redcoats and Loyalists loaded onto the last of the British ships. They left New York on November 25, 1783. As the British set sail for England, Washington triumphantly led eight hundred Continental officers and soldiers into New York City. No free Continental soldier had set foot in that city for seven years.

Battling overwhelming hardships and a superior enemy, the Americans easily could have given up. But against all odds, the unpaid, freezing, starving army held together. Through the horrific winters, the heated battles, the turmoil of treason, and the storms of mutiny, these brave men never lost their fierce determination to be free.

Washington, reflecting on all the hardships his men had endured, wrote to his brother John, "That men under these circumstances were held together is hardly within the bounds of credibility, but is nevertheless true."

When the war ended, General Washington expressed the highest praise for the troops in his farewell address:

> *"The unparalleled perseverance of the Armies of the United States, through almost every possible suffering and discouragement, for the space of eight long years, was little short of a standing miracle."*

FOR MORE about the Battle of Yorktown, go to the Mount Vernon website at www.mountvernon.org and search for "Now or Never," a series of short videos about the battle.

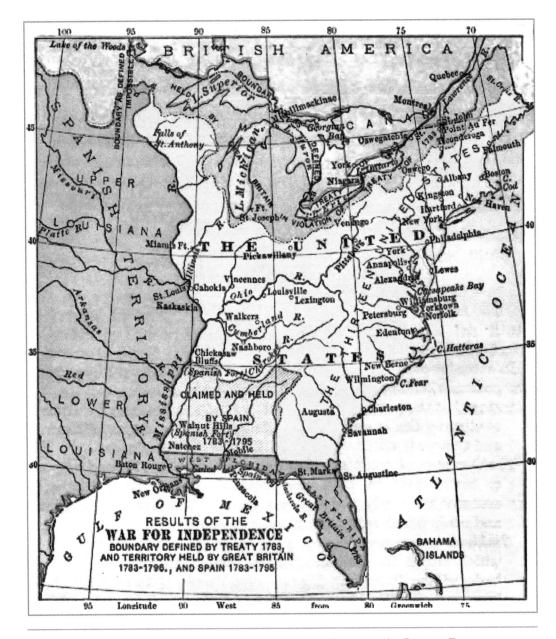

RESULTS OF THE
WAR FOR INDEPENDENCE
BOUNDARY DEFINED BY TREATY 1783,
AND TERRITORY HELD BY GREAT BRITAIN
1783-1796., AND SPAIN 1783-1795

TERRITORIES GRANTED TO THE UNITED STATES (YELLOW), GREAT BRITAIN (PINK), AND SPAIN (GREEN), AS A RESULT OF THE TREATY OF PARIS. GREAT BRITAIN HELD ONTO THE GREAT LAKES AREA IN VIOLATION OF THE TREATY (ORANGE), BUT THE UNITED STATES DROVE THE BRITISH OUT IN 1795.

GALLERY OF HEROES

JOSEPH PLUMB MARTIN was born in Becket, Massachusetts, and grew up on his grandfather's farm. Young Joseph was a strong, hard-working farm boy. He lacked a formal education but learned to read and loved reading.

When the Revolution began, Martin enlisted for six months. He was only 15 and too young to enlist without his parents' consent, but the enlistment agents didn't ask questions. At the end of his term, he reenlisted for the duration of the war. Private Martin fought in most of the major battles. In 1780, he was assigned to an engineering unit and promoted to Sergeant.

After the war, Martin settled down in Frankfort (now Prospect), Maine. He and his wife Lucy raised five children. He farmed and worked as the town clerk for twenty-five

THERE ARE NO KNOWN PICTURES OF JOSEPH MARTIN. THE ABOVE ILLUSTRATION REPRESENTS A TYPICAL CONTINENTAL SOLDIER.

years. Throughout his life, Martin read the classics and history books. He also wrote church hymns.

At 69, the old soldier wrote a book about his wartime memories. He said he wrote it to avoid the trouble of retelling his stories so often. His wrote in a friendly style with a natural wit. Historians consider Martin's book, *Narrative of Some of the Adventures, Dangers and Sufferings of a Revolutionary Soldier*, the most complete account of the Revolution by a foot soldier. Joseph Plumb Martin enjoyed life for 89 years.

JAMES THACHER grew up on a farm near Barnstable, Massachusetts. At 16, he studied medicine with a local doctor. The slightly built young doctor was 21 when he joined the Continental Army.

Dr. Thacher traveled with the troops to the major battlefields and cared for the wounded. Between battles, he kept a journal. His writing shows his patriotism and his respect for the soldiers. Today experts recognize Thacher's book, *Military Journal of the American Revolution*, as one of the most reliable eyewitness accounts of the war.

Dr. Thacher was 29 when the war ended. He returned to Massachusetts as an experienced surgeon and settled in Plymouth. There he and his wife Susannah raised two daughters. He practiced medicine, taught medicine, and wrote medical books. Thacher's national standing as a medical scholar grew. He also wrote about other subjects, including history, ghosts, and raising bees.

At 70, Dr. Thacher helped found the Pilgrim Society. The Society's purpose is to preserve the pilgrims' story. As you know, the pilgrims sailed to America in 1620 looking for religious freedom, and landed at Plymouth Rock. The Pilgrim Society built Pilgrim Hall Museum in 1824. James Thacher proudly served as the Museum's first librarian.

The good doctor lived to be 91.

You can visit Pilgrim Hall and read about the Pilgrims at www.pilgrimhall.org.

NATHANAEL GREENE was born in Rhode Island into a Quaker family. Nathanael, a tall and strong young man, worked in his father's mills and iron forge. He had no formal schooling, but read books whenever he found time. He was by nature organized and taught himself many subjects.

Greene joined the Continental Army when he was 34. The Quaker religion disapproved of wars, but Greene was not a typical Quaker. He fought intensely throughout the Revolution. In 1780, Washington thought Greene was his best general and appointed him Commander of the Southern Army. The outcome of the Revolution rested directly on the "fighting Quaker's" shoulders. Greene's well-planned strategy to harass and wear down the British—he famously described it as, "We fight, get beat, rise and fight again"—made victory at Yorktown possible.

After the war, Greene, his wife "Caty," and their five children moved to Georgia. That state had awarded him a grand plantation called Mulberry Grove to thank him for driving out the British. One hot day in Georgia, General Greene became ill during a long horseback ride in the blistering sun. It is assumed that he suffered heatstroke. Nathanael Greene died on July 19, 1786. He was only 44 years old.

Today, historians agree with Washington; Major General Nathanael Greene was his best general. Countless U.S. towns, counties, streets, schools and more are named in Greene's honor.

More information about General Greene and his home, Spell Hall, can be found at www.nathanaelgreenehomestead.org.

ANTHONY WAYNE grew up in Chester County, Pennsylvania. Young Anthony liked to dig trenches and stage battles with his friends. He was educated at a private academy in Philadelphia. He and his wife Polly raised two children in his childhood home, called Waynesborough.

Wayne was 31 when he joined the Continental Army. Early in the Revolution, one unhappy soldier thought Wayne's punishments were too severe, and tagged him "Mad Anthony Wayne." It stuck. The bold and fiery General is best remembered for his daring capture of Stoney Point. At the end of the war, Georgia presented the General with a large rice plantation to express gratitude for reclaiming that state.

After the war, Wayne served in government for a few years. But in 1792, his country needed him again. President Washington appointed Wayne commander of a new American Army. His orders were to remove the Native American tribes and the British from the Ohio Territory. The tribes, with British support, were terrorizing and killing settlers.

In three years, Wayne created an impressive army, crushed the tribes, forced the British out of the Great Lakes forts, and negotiated peace. This campaign opened up the wild frontier for safe and peaceful

ANTHONY WAYNE BY JAMES SHARPLES SENIOR, FROM LIFE, 1796

settlements. The population of the territory increased rapidly. Ohio was admitted into the Union as the 17th state in 1803. Winning the Ohio Territory is considered Wayne's greatest legacy. Many places in the Eastern and Midwestern states are named in honor of Wayne, indicating the importance of his success in the Ohio Territory

Major General Anthony Wayne died of an illness at 51.

To learn more about the General and his home, visit http://historicwaynesborough.org.

LORD STIRLING, WILLIAM ALEXANDER, was born on Christmas Day, 1726, into a wealthy New York family and was well educated. As a young man, Alexander briefly lived in Great Britain where he filed a claim for the vacant Scottish title of Earl of Stirling.

Although the British House of Lords failed to recognize his claim, Americans called him Lord Stirling anyway. The rebel colonists liked having a "British Lord" leading their fight for freedom from Britain.

Lord Stirling built a country mansion near Basking Ridge, New Jersey, where he and his wife Sarah raised two daughters. Stirling was an enthusiastic man. He spent money freely, sometimes using his own funds to pay for war expenses.

Stirling was 48 years old when he joined the Continental Army and commanded the New Jersey Line. He had gained military experience as an officer in the militia. The brave officer is best remembered for his heroic actions during the Battle of Long Island. He and 250 Marylanders held a defensive stand against thousands of British troops, allowing the main American Army to escape. Stirling and fewer than a dozen Maryland soldiers survived. The General was captured, but later released in a prisoner exchange. After the Battle of Long Island, no one ever questioned Lord Stirling's bravery. Washington, who always addressed him as "My Lord," trusted and valued him.

Although his health was declining, Major General Lord Stirling was still in the army when he died, just months before the Treaty of Paris was signed. He was 57 years old.

Lord Stirling Park in Basking Ridge, New Jersey, is located on part of his former estate.

FIRST NATIONAL HISTORICAL PARK

Morristown National Historical Park was the first National Historical Park in the United States. The Park officially opened to the public on July 4, 1933.

Today, Morristown National Historical Park includes: the Ford Mansion, Washington's Headquarters Museum and Library, Jockey Hollow Encampment Area including the soldiers' huts and the Wick House, New Jersey Brigade Encampment Area, Cross Estate Gardens, and Fort Nonsense.

Fort Nonsense is a park on the highest hilltop in Morristown. During the Revolution, the Fort provided an excellent location for a lookout post and a signal beacon. It also served as a storage depot. It's called Fort Nonsense because, in the 1800's, the residents didn't understand its purpose. The name stuck.

On a snowy day, the 240-year old Ford Mansion in Morristown and the Wick house and fields in Jockey Hollow look much as they did when the Continental Army first saw them in 1779.

When you visit, walk in the Jockey Hollow soldiers' footsteps. Be awed by their courage and perseverance. And let their victory, against all odds, inspire you.

REENACTMENT OF THE CONTINENTAL ARMY MUSTERING AT
YORKTOWN BATTLEFIELD, VIRGINIA

TIME LINE OF EVENTS

1775 APRIL 19. Redcoats and Minutemen fight the Battles of Lexington and Concord, Massachusetts.

MAY 10. The Green Mountain Boys, a militia unit led by Ethan Allen and Benedict Arnold, capture Fort Ticonderoga, New York.

JUNE 17. Colonial soldiers battle the British at Bunker Hill near Boston.

DECEMBER 30-31. American forces under Benedict Arnold fail to seize Quebec, Canada.

1776 JULY 4. Congress adopts the Declaration of Independence.

AUGUST 27. British are victorious in the Battle of Long Island. The Continental Army escapes during a thick fog. Redcoats push the Continentals out of New York, across New Jersey, and into Pennsylvania.

SEPTEMBER 15. British set up headquarters in New York City.

DECEMBER 26. Washington surprises the enemy at Trenton, New Jersey by crossing the Delaware River on Christmas night and attacking at dawn.

1777 JANUARY 3. Continentals are victorious in a surprise attack at Princeton, New Jersey.

JUNE 13. Lafayette arrives in America and volunteers to fight with the Continentals.

SEPTEMBER 11. British win the Battle of Brandywine, Pennsylvania, and move their headquarters to Philadelphia.

OCTOBER 17. Continentals and Militias win a major victory at Saratoga, New York.

DECEMBER. Continental Soldiers march to winter camp at Valley Forge, Pennsylvania.

1778 JUNE 18. British move their headquarters back to New York City.

JUNE 28. Continentals and Militias fight the British at Monmouth Courthouse in New Jersey.

DECEMBER 2. British capture and occupy Savannah, Georgia for four years.

1779 JULY 15 – 16. Anthony Wayne and his daring troops capture the fort at Stoney Point, New York.

AUGUST 19. Harry Lee captures the fort at Paulus Hook, New Jersey.

NOVEMBER – DECEMBER. Continental soldiers march to winter camp at Jockey Hollow. It is the harshest winter of the century.

1780 MAY 12. British win the battle at Charlestown, South Carolina, and take all American troops as prisoners. It is the Americans' worst defeat of the war.

JUNE 7. British troops invade New Jersey in an attempt to destroy the Continental Army and supplies at Morristown. They battle regular and militia soldiers at Connecticut Farms. Redcoats retreat during the night.

JUNE 23. Again, Redcoats set out for Morristown to blow up American supplies and ammunitions. They battle at Springfield. Again they retreat. It is the last British invasion in the North.

AUGUST 16. Commanding General Horatio Gates abandons the battlefield and the Continentals suffer a devastating defeat at Camden, South Carolina.

SEPTEMBER 23. Militiamen capture John André and uncover Benedict Arnold's treason.

OCTOBER 4. Washington names Nathanael Greene Commander of the Southern Army.

OCTOBER 7. Patriot militias defeat Loyalist militias at King's Mountain, South Carolina.

1781 JANUARY 1. Pennsylvania Line mutinies over terms of enlistment, back pay, lack of food and clothing. After accepting settlement terms, most return to serve until the war's end.

JANUARY 17. Daniel Morgan wins an overwhelming victory at Cowpens, South Carolina.

MARCH 15. Redcoats battle Greene's troops and militias at Guilford Courthouse, North Carolina. British claim victory but the battle costs them too many lives.

MARCH – JUNE. British hold off Greene's attacks at Ninety-Six, South Carolina.

SEPTEMBER 15. French fleet and ground troops arrive at Chesapeake Bay and drive the British navy out of the bay. British supply lines are cut off.

OCTOBER 19. British surrender to the French-American allies at Yorktown, Virginia.

1782 JULY 11. Wayne and his men drive the Redcoats from Savannah, Georgia.

DECEMBER 14. Greene and Wayne force the British from Charleston, South Carolina.

1783 SEPTEMBER 3. United States of America and Great Britain sign the Treaty of Paris.

NOVEMBER 25. British leave New York City. Washington and 800 Continentals enter the city and reclaim it for America.

PLACES TO EXPLORE

Websites to explore for facts and images related to the Revolutionary War.

COLONIAL WILLIAMSBURG. www.history.org. Witness history in an authentic colonial town, select "Tour the Town" for an interactive map of the village. See webcam views of Williamsburg's historic buildings. Select "Kids" then "games and activities" to write with a quill pen, design and send an e-postcard to a friend, and lots more.

FRIENDS OF MONMOUTH BATTLEFIELD. www.friendsofmonmouth. org. Each year the Friends, along with others, co-sponsor a reenactment of the battle. Click "Annual Reenactment of the Battle of Monmouth, June 20-21, 2015" to see photos of the event.

GREAT SWAMP. www.fws.gov/refuge/Great_Swamp. Learn about this twelve square mile natural oasis and wildlife refuge that protected the Jockey Hollow encampment from the British in 1780.

MOUNT VERNON, WASHINGTON'S HOME. www.mountvernon.org. Go to "Educational Resources" then click "For Students" for a virtual tour and videos including "Winter Patriots" and "Now or Never." For fun, search for "George's Big Day Out," a video of Washington time-traveling in modern Washington D.C.

OLD BARRACKS. www.barracks.org. The Old Barracks served as officers' quarters during the Revolution. When Washington and the Continentals attacked Trenton in 1776, enemy soldiers were quartered there. Be sure to watch the "New Old Barracks" video.

TRENT HOUSE. www.williamtrenthouse.org. William Trent built Trent House in 1719. Enemy officers occupied Trent House in 1776. Now it's a museum dedicated to providing a basic understanding of life in the 1700's. Take a virtual tour of this very old house.

U. S. GOVERNMENT'S OFFICIAL WEB PORTAL FOR KIDS. www.Kids.gov. "Learn stuff, play games, watch videos," covering a wide range of topics.

WASHINGTON ASSOCIATION OF NEW JERSEY. www.wanj.org. WANJ supports Morristown National Historical Park in preserving and interpreting the site and honors Washington and his troops. Check out photos of the park and videos, including "Morristown, Where America Survived."

WASHINGTON CROSSING HISTORIC PARK. www.washingtoncrossingpark.org. Click "The Park" and select "Crossing Reenactment" to view a video of reenactors crossing the Delaware River. Select "The Village" for more information about the Durham flat bottomed boats that Washington and his men used.

National Park Service (NPS) websites

"Learn about the Park" is a good place to start exploring each NPS site.

COLONIAL NATIONAL HISTORICAL PARK AND YORKTOWN BATTLEFIELD. www.nps.gov/colo. Find facts and photos about the Battle of Yorktown.

COWPENS NATIONAL BATTLEFIELD. www.nps.gov/cowp. Learn more about General Morgan's "double envelope" battle plan.

FORT MOULTRIE is a unit of Fort Sumter National Monument. www.nps.gov/fosu.

GUILFORD COURTHOUSE NATIONAL MILITARY PARK. www.nps.gov/guco.

KINGS MOUNTAIN NATIONAL MILITARY PARK. www.nps.gov/kimo.

MINUTE MAN NATIONAL HISTORICAL PARK. www.nps.gov/mima.

MORRISTOWN NATIONAL HISTORICAL PARK. www.nps.gov/morr.

NATIONAL PARK SERVICE AMERICAN REVOLUTION. www.nps.gov/revwar. Select "Who, What, When" for a detailed Revolutionary War timeline, as well as stories, people, and more.

SARATOGA NATIONAL HISTORICAL PARK. www.nps.gov/sara.

VALLEY FORGE NATIONAL HISTORICAL PARK. www.nps.gov/vafo.

To find a National Park near you, visit www.nps.gov, click "Find a Park" and select your state.

Resources for Teachers

COLONIAL WILLIAMSBURG. www.history.org. Check out the Education, Multimedia, and Kids drop-down menus for teacher resources. And for more about the features of Williamsburg's HERO online programming, go to www.colonialwilliamsburg.org/hero.

MOUNT VERNON. www.mountvernon.org. Click "Educational Resources," then "For Teachers." The website lists lesson plans, materials, DVDs, videos and more as available resources.

NATIONAL PARK SERVICE AMERICAN REVOLUTION. www.nps.gov/revwar. Select "Educational Resources" then "Teachers".

U.S. GOVERNMENT'S OFFICIAL WEB PORTAL FOR KIDS. www.Kids.gov. Click "Teachers" for activities, worksheets, and lesson plans on an extensive range of topics—according to the website, the most popular topics are fitness, science, social studies, and jobs.

ADDITIONAL READING

Castrovilla, Selene. *By the Sword*. Honesdale, Pennsylvania: Calkins Creek, 2007.

Fradin, Dennis Brindell. *The Battle of Yorktown*. New York: Marshall Cavendish Benchmark, 2009.

Freedman, Russell. *Washington at Valley Forge*. New York: Holiday House, 2008.

Freedman, Russell. *Lafayette and the American Revolution*. New York: Holiday House, 2010.

Hakim, Joy. *A History of US: From Colonies to Country: 1735-1791*. New York: Oxford University Press, 1993.

Mierka, Gregg A. *Nathanael Greene, The General Who Saved the Revolution*. Stockton, New Jersey: OTTN Publishing, 2007.

Murphy, Jim. *A Young Patriot, The American Revolution as Experienced by One Boy*. New York: Scholastic Inc., 1997.

Peacock, Louise. *Crossing the Delaware, a History in Many Voices.* New York: Scholastic, Inc., 1999.

Yoder, Carolyn P., ed. *George Washington the Writer.* Honesdale, Pennsylvania: Boyds Mills Press, 2003.

Advanced Reading
Bober, Natalie S. *Abigail Adams, Witness to a Revolution.* New York: Aladdin Paperbacks, 1998.

Bohrer, Melissa Lukeman. *Glory, Passion, and Principle: The Story of Eight Remarkable Women at the Core of the American Revolution.* New York: Atria Books, 2003

Cunningham, John T. *The Uncertain Revolution, Washington & the Continental Army at Morristown.* West Creek, New Jersey: Cormorant Publishing, 2007.

Diamant, Lincoln. *Chaining the Hudson, the Fight for the River in the American Revolution.* New York: Carol Publishing Group, 1994.

Fleming, Thomas. *How Mad Anthony Won the West.* New Word City, Inc., 2011.

Fleming, Thomas. *Liberty! The American Revolution.* New York: Viking Penguin, 1997.

Magill, Arthur. *Battle at the Cowpens.* Greenville, South Carolina: The Reedy River Press, Inc., 1980.

CREDITS AND BIBLIOGRAPHY

CHAPTER 1 - WEATHER

"[We] reached this wilderness . . . ,"
James Thacher, *Military Journal
of the American Revolution* (Boston:
Richardson & Lord, 1823), Nook
e-book, 159.

"Our lodging . . . last night . . . ," Ibid.

"Our march lasted six days . . . ,"
Friedrich Kapp, *Life of John Kalb* (New
York: Henry Holt and Company, 1884),
Nook e-book, 129.

"one of the most tremendous
snowstorms . . . ," Thacher, *Military
Journal,* 162.

"Ink freezes in my pen," Kapp, *Life of
John Kalb,* 130.

"Those who have only been to Valley
Forge . . . ," Ibid.

CHAPTER 2 - SHELTER

"Since the beginning of this month . . .
," Ibid.

"The sufferings of the poor soldiers . . .
," Thacher, *Military Journal,* 162-163.

"When digging just below the frost,"
Joseph Plumb Martin, *Memoir of a
Revolutionary Soldier* (Hallowell, Maine:
Glazier, Masters & Co.) 1830. Print
reproduction, Dover Publications, Inc.,
(Mineola, New York, 2006). 94.

"We have now the satisfaction . . . ,"
Thacher, *Military Journal,* 167.

"Eighteen [servants] belonging to my
family . . . ," John C. Fitzpatrick, ed.,
The George Washington Papers, Library
of Congress, Manuscript Division, GW
(George Washington) to Nathanael
Greene, January 22, 1780.

"The poor General was so unhappy . . . ," Patricia Brady, *Martha Washington: An American Life* (NYC: Viking Penguin, 2005), Nook e-book, 135.

CHAPTER 3 - SUPPLIES
"We were absolutely, literally starved . . . ," Martin, *Memoir,* 97.

"We are frequently for six to eight days . . . ," Thacher, *Military Journal,* 163.

"thin enough to have straws shot through . . . ," Martin, *Memoir,* 161.

"They mean to leave us . . . ," Anthony Wayne to William Irvine, Dec. 14, 1779, History Magazine, VI (October 1862), 322, quoted in George F. Scheer and Hugh F. Rankin, *Rebels and Redcoats* (New York: World Publication Company, 1957). USA: Da Capo Press, Inc., Print Reproduction, n. d., 367. Copyright © 08-22-1987 books-contributor-hugh-20f-20rankin. Reprinted by permission of Da Capo, a member of the Perseus Books Group.

"The situation of the army. . . ," Fitzpatrick, *Washington Papers,* GW to Governor Clinton, December 16, 1779.

CHAPTER 3 SIDEBAR - GRUMBLING

"An ordinary horse . . . ," Kapp, *Life of John Kalb,* 131.

"Trash." Thacher, *Military Journal,* 170.

"I had 2 or 3 shillings . . . ," Martin, *Memoir,* 87.

"a rat in the shape . . . ," Fitzpatrick, *Washington Papers,* GW to Gouverneur Morris, October 4, 1778.

"A hat costs four . . . ," Kapp, *Life of John Kalb,* 130.

CHAPTER 4 - MANPOWER

"This was what has been termed . . . ," Martin, *Memoir,* 95.

"An iron constitution . . . ," Kapp, *Life of John Kalb,* 130.

"Our poor soldiers . . . ," Thacher, *Military Journal,* 173.

"We were unwilling to desert . . . ," Martin, *Memoir,* 105.

"Our troops in camp . . . ," Thacher, *Military Journal,* 178.

CHAPTER 5 - BATTLES

"The people are arming and training . . . ," *Nicholas Cresswell, The Journal of Nicholas Cresswell, 1774 – 1777,* with permission from Applewood Books, (Carlisle, Massachusetts: Applewood Books, 1924). 57.

"Our officers and men behaved . . . ," *Charles Janeway Stillé, Major-General Anthony Wayne and the Pennsylvania Line in the Continental Army* (Philadelphia: J. B. Lippencott, 1893). USA: British Library, Print Reproduction, n.d., 196.

"At 6 o'clock in the morning . . . ," Thacher, *Military Journal,* 176.

"Colonel Angell's regiment . . . ," Ibid.

"Put Watts in 'em, boys." Washington Irving, *Life of Washington,* vol. 3 (New York: Thomas Y. Crowell and Company, 1900), 230.

"They [the British] are directing their . . . ," Fitzpatrick, *Washington Papers,* Nathanael Greene to GW, June 23, 1780.

"Our troops were commanded . . . ," Thacher, *Military Journal,* 177.

CHAPTER 6 - TREASON

"Treason, of the blackest . . . ," Fitzpatrick, *Washington Papers,* General Orders, Nathanael Greene, September 26, 1780.

"It was reported that General Arnold . . . ," Martin, *Memoir,* 115.
"The merit of this gentleman . . . ," Fitzpatrick, *Washington Papers,* GW to Philip J. Schuyler, December 5, 1775.

"All is safe and I again . . . ," Samuel W. Pennypacker, *Anthony Wayne* (Philadelphia: J. B. Lippencott, 1908), Nook e-book, 22. *Anthony Wayne* is a transcript of Pennypacker's address at Valley Forge on June 30, 1908, during the dedication of the equestrian statue of Major General Wayne. The address was prepared from original letters in the Library of the Historical Society of Pennsylvania. Source notes were not included in the transcription.

"The pages of our history . . . ," Thacher, *Military Journal,* 190.

CHAPTER 7 - MUTINY

"by their sufferings . . . ," Fitzpatrick, *Washington Papers,* GW letter to Governor George Clinton, February 16, 1778.

"About two hundred soldiers . . . ," Thacher, *Military Journal,* 166.

"growling like soreheaded dogs," Martin, *Memoir,* 103.

"They saw no other alternative . . . ," Ibid, 103.

"This matter . . . has given . . . , Fitzpatrick, *Washington Papers,* GW to Continental Congress, May 27, 1780.

"Indeed, I have almost ceased to hope," Fitzpatrick, *Washington Papers,* GW to Joseph Reed, May 28, 1780.

"They [the Pennsylvania Line] have now served their country . . . ," Anthony Wayne to Joseph Reed, December 16, 1780. William B. Reed, ed., *Life and Correspondence of Joseph Reed,* Vol. 2, (Philadelphia: Lindsay and Blakiston, 1847). Print reproduction, Nabu Press, n.d. 315-7.

"Arnolds," Stillé, *Major-General Anthony Wayne,* 247.

"We love you, we respect you . . . ," Ibid, 243.

"It is in vain to think . . . ," Fitzpatrick, *Washington Papers,* GW to Meshech Weare, et al, January 5, 1781, Circular Letter on Pennsylvania Line Mutiny.

"I hope [in] a few weeks . . . ," Fitzpatrick, *Washington Papers,* Anthony Wayne to GW, January 21, 1781.

"a most unfortunate transaction, . . . ," Thacher, *Military Journal,* 220.

"If you succeed in compelling . . . ," Fitzpatrick, *Washington Papers,* GW to Robert Howe, January 22, 1781

CHAPTER 8 – PERSEVERANCE

"Huzza for the Americans!" Martin, *Memoir,* 132.

"the tiptoe of expectation . . . ," Ibid.

"About noon, the much-wished-for . . . ," Ibid.

"General Washington put the match . . . ," Thacher, *Military Journal,* 249.

"From the 10th to the 15th . . . ," Ibid.

"slow and solemn," Ibid, 254.

"very unofficer like manner . . . ," Ibid.

"the officers and soldiers . . . ," Scheer and Rankin, *Rebels & Redcoats,* 495. Copyright © 08-22-1987 books-contributor-hugh-20f-20rankin. Reprinted by permission of Da Capo, a member of the Perseus Books Group.

"There was as much sorrow as joy . . . ," Martin, *Memoir,* 159.

"ties of brotherly affection," Thacher, *Military Journal,* 287.

"one patriotic band of Brothers . . . ," Fitzpatrick, *Washington Papers,* Farewell Orders to Armies of the U.S., November 2, 1783.

"That men under these circumstances . . . ," Fitzpatrick, *Washington Papers.* This quote is from a letter that Washington wrote to his brother John. He began the letter on June 6, 1780, but was interrupted by the Battle at Connecticut Farms. He wrote the second half of the letter, including the quote, on July 6, 1780.

"The unparalleled perseverance of the Armies . . . ," Fitzpatrick, *Washington Papers,* Farewell Orders to Armies of the U.S., November 2, 1783.

GALLERY OF HEROES

Nathanael Greene
"We fight, get beat, rise and fight again," Sheer and Rankin, *Rebels & Redcoats,* 465. Copyright © 08-22-1987 books-contributor-hugh-20f-20rankin. Reprinted by permission of Da Capo, a member of the Perseus Books Group.

IMAGE CREDITS

The author gratefully acknowledges that the images in this book are used through the courtesy of the persons and institutions listed below.

American Revolution Photos, www.americanrrevolutionphotos.com: 42, 48, 54.

David Gruol Photography: 21 (all), 22 (all), 73, 96 (all).

Encore Editions, "Surrender of Lord Cornwallis," John Trumbull: 82.

Fraunces Tavern® Museum, New York City, "Battle of Springfield, New Jersey, 1780," John Ward Dunsmore: 52.

Grafton, John, *The American Revolution, A Picture Source Book,* Mineola, New York: Dover Publications, Inc., 1975: 27, 30, 41, 61, 67, 85, 89, 91.

Granger Collection, New York City, "Battle of Fort Moultrie, 1776," 46 (top), "Mutiny: Anthony Wayne, 1781," 69.

Library of Congress, Prints and Photographs Division, Popular Graphic Arts Collection, "Evacuation Day and Washington's Triumphal Entry In New York City, November 25, 1783:" LC-DIG-pga-02468: 86.

Lossing, Benson J., *A Pictorial Field Book of the Revolution,* 2 volumes, New York: Harper & Brothers, Publishers, 1860. Last accessed online on March 2, 2015, http://freepages.history. rootswebancestry.com/~wcarr/ Lossing1/Front.html: 17, 32, 33, 36, 50, 63, 94.

National Park Service, Independence National Historical Park: "Anthony Wayne," James Sharples Senior, from life, 1796, INDE11922: 93.

National Park Service, Museum Management Program and Morristown National Historical Park, "Map of Morristown, NJ," MORRmap, origin unknown: 13.

North Wind Picture Archives Color: Front Cover, 2, 10, 14, 18, 25, 28, 34, 38, 56, 62, 64, 70, 74, 76, 80, 98.

The Society of the Sons of the Revolution in the State of Virginia: 83.

U. S. Army Medical Department Office of Medical History Website, http://history.amedd.army.mil/booksdocs/misc/evprev/ch3.htm, last accessed March 3, 2015, images include United States Government works, (17 USC 403): 40 (all).

US History Images, http://ushistoryimages.com: Wayne's Medal, Lossing, Benson J. *Harper's Encyclopedia of United States History.*" New York: Harper and Brothers Publishers, 1912. 45.
Arnold at Saratoga, Jones, J. R. *American History for Young Folks: the Story of Our Great Country.* 1898. 59.
Map of America in 1783, McMaster, John Bach. A School History of the United States. New York: American Book Company. 1897. 88.

Wikimedia Commons/Public Domain: 8, 79, 90.

Writer's collection, photographs by David Lauerman: 16, 24, 46 (bottom), 55, Back Cover.

BIBLIOGRAPHY
Primary Sources

Cresswell, Nicholas. *The Journal of Nicholas Cresswell,* 1774-1777. New York: The Dial Press, 1924. Carlisle, Massachusetts: Applewood Books, 1924, Print Reproduction, n.d.

Fitzpatrick, John C., ed. *The Writings of George Washington from the Original Manuscript Sources,* 1745-1799. Library of Congress, Manuscript Division. http://memory.loc.gov. Accessed March 18, 2015.

Martin, Joseph Plumb. *Memoir of a Revolutionary Soldier, the Narrative of Joseph Plumb Martin.* Hallowell, Maine: Glazier, Masters & Company, 1830. Print Reproduction, Dover Publications, Inc.,Mineola, New York, 2006.

Reed, William B., ed. *Life and Correspondence of Joseph Reed,* Vol. 2, (Philadelphia: Lindsay and Blakiston, 1847). Print reproduction, Nabu Press, n.d.

Taylor, C. James, ed. *The Adams Papers Digital Edition.* Charlottesville: University of Virginia, Rotunda, 2008. http://rotunda.upress.virginia.edu/founders/ADMS-06-12-02-0059. Accessed July 30, 2012. Original source: Papers of John Adams, Vol.12, October 1781 – April 1782.

Thacher, James, M.D. *Military Journal during the American Revolutionary War, 1775 to 1783,* Boston: Richardson & Lord, 1823. Nook e-book, digital reproduction made available by Internet Archive.

Secondary Sources - Books

Babits, Lawrence E. *A Devil of a Whipping the Battle of Cowpens.* Chapel Hill: The University of North Carolina Press, 1998.

Bakeless, John. *Turncoats, Traitors & Heroes, Espionage in the American Revolution.* New York: J. B. Lippincott, 1959. New York: Da Capo Press, Inc., Print Reproduction, 1998.

Bohrer, Melissa Lukeman. *Glory, Passion, and Principle: The Story of Eight Remarkable Women at the Core of the American Revolution.* New York: Atria Books, 2003.

Brady, Patricia. *Martha Washington: an American Life.* New York: Viking Penguin, 2005. Nook e-book.

Buchanan, John. *The Road to Guilford Courthouse.* New York: John Wiley & Sons, Inc., 1997.

Chernow, Ron. *Washington, a Life.* New York: Penguin Press, 2010.

Commager, Henry Steele and Richard B. Morris, ed. *The Spirit of Seventy-Six.* 2nd ed. Edison, New Jersey: Castle Books, 2002.

Cunningham, John T. *The Uncertain Revolution, Washington & the Continental Army at Morristown.* West Creek, New Jersey: Cormorant Publishing, 2007.

Diamant, Lincoln. *Chaining the Hudson, the Fight for the River in the American Revolution.* New York: Carol Publishing Group, 1994.

Duer, William Alexander. *The Life of William Alexander, Earl of Stirling.* New York: Wiley & Putnam, 1847. Charleston: BiblioBazaar, Print Reproduction, 2011.

Ellis, Joseph J. *His Excellency, George Washington.* New York: Vintage Books, 2005.

Ferling, John. *Almost a Miracle, the American Victory in the War of Independence.* New York: Oxford University Press, 2007.

Fischer, David Hackett. *Washington's Crossing.* New York: Oxford University Press, 2004.

Fleming, Thomas J. "Downright Fighting." *Cowpens National Battlefield Park Handbook* 135. Washington, D. C.: U. S. Department of the Interior, National Park Service, Division of Publications, 1988.

Fleming, Thomas. *The Forgotten Victory, the Battle for New Jersey – 1780.* New York: Reader's Digest Press, 1973.

_____. *How Mad Anthony Wayne Won the West.* New Word City, Inc., 2011. Nook e-book.

_____. *Liberty! The American Revolution.* New York: Viking Penguin, 1997.

Higgenbotham, Don. *Daniel Morgan Revolutionary Rifleman.* Chapel Hill: The University of North Carolina Press, 1961.

Irving, Washington. *Life of Washington,* vols. 3 & 4. Carlisle, Massachusetts: Thomas Y. Crowell and Company, 1900.

Kapp, Friedrich. *Life of John Kalb.* New York: Henry Holt and Company, 1884. Nook e-book, digital reproduction made available by the Internet Archive.

Lossing, Benson J. *A Pictorial Field Book of the Revolution,* vols. 1 & 2. New York: Harper & Brothers, Publishers, 1860. Accessed March 2, 2015. http://freepages.history.rootswebancestry.com/~wcarr/Lossing1/Front.html.

Magill, Arthur. *Battle at the Cowpens.* Greenville, South Caroline: The Reedy River Press, Inc., 1980.

Mayers, Robert A. *The War Man.* Yardley, Pennsylvania: Westholme Publishing, 2009.

McCullough, David. *1776*. New York: Simon & Schuster, 2006.

McMaster, John Bach. *A School History of the United States*. New York: American Book Company, 1897.

Mitnick, Barbara J., ed. *New Jersey in the American Revolution*. New Brunswick, New Jersey: Rivergate Books, 2005.

Nelson, Paul David. *The Life of William Alexander, Lord Stirling*. University, Alabama: The University of Alabama Press, 1987.

Pennypacker, Samuel W. *Anthony Wayne*. Philadelphia: J. B. Lippencott, 1908. Nook e-book, digital reproduction made available by the Internet Archive.

Pfister, Jude M. *The Jacob Ford Jr. Mansion, the Storied History of a New Jersey Home*. Charleston, South Carolina: The History Press, 2009.

Scheer, George F. and Hugh F. Rankin. *Rebels & Redcoats*. New York: World Publishing Company, 1957. USA: Da Capo Press, Inc., Print Reproduction, n.d.

Stillé, Charles Janeway. *Major-General Anthony Wayne and the Pennsylvania Line in the Continental Army*. Philadelphia: J. B. Lippencott, 1893. USA: British Library, Print Reproduction, n.d.

Tonsetic, Robert L. 1781, *The Decisive Year of the Revolutionary War*. Havertown, PA: Casemate Publishers, 2013.

Van Doren, Carl. *Mutiny in January*. New York: The Viking Press, 1943.

Weig, Melvin J. *Morristown National Historical Park Handbook* 7. Washington, D. C.: U. S. Department of the Interior, National Park Service, Government Printing Office, 1950.

Weigley, Russell Frank and George F. Scheer. *Morristown Official National Park Handbook* 120. Washington, D. C.: U. S. Department of the Interior, National Park Service, Division of Publications, 1983.

Secondary Sources – Articles and Web Sites

"After the 'Hard Winter': June 1780." *Morris Muster – Newsletter of Morristown National Historical Park*. Summer 2011.

Crannell, W. W. "The Youngest Soldier of the Revolution." *St. Nicholas: an Illustrated Magazine for Young Folks.* Mary Mapes Dodge, ed. Vol. 11, Part 2, May to October, 1884. NY: The Century Company, 1884. 697-700. Lexington, KY: University of Michigan, Print Reproduction, 2012.

Ellet, Elizabeth F. "Women of the American Revolution." *AmericanRevolution.org.* http://www.americanrevolution.org/women/women44.html. Accessed April 28, 2012.

"Events Leading to the Siege of Yorktown, 1781." *National Park Service, Yorktown National Battlefield.* http://www.nps.gov/york/historyculture/eventstoyorktown.htm. Accessed February 26, 2012.

Flowers, Charles. "The Long Road to Victory." *WNC Magazine.* http://www.wncmagazine.com. Accessed July 31, 2012.

"Fort Nonsense," and "New Jersey Brigade and Cross Estate Gardens." *National Park Service, Morristown National Historical Park,* http://www.nps.gov/morr/learn/historyculture/fortnonsense.htm. Accessed May 22, 2015.

"Mad Anthony Wayne, an American Genius." T*he Legion Ville Historical Society, Inc.* 1996. This website is no longer available; a downloaded copy can be provided.

"Morristown, Where America Survived, the People, Richard Lord Jones." *New Jersey Public Television and Radio.* Accessed February 2, 2012. This website is no longer available; a downloaded copy can be provided.

"Office of Medical History, Surgeons General, James Tilton." *U. S. Medical Department.* http://history.amedd.army.mil/surgeongenerals/J_Tilton.html. Accessed March 3, 2015.

"Part III, The American Revolutionary War and First Years of the Republic (1775-1783, 1799); Establishment of the Medical Department of the Army, James Tilton (1745-1822); Rules for Prevention of Diseases." *U. S. Army Medical Department.* http://history.amedd.army.mil/booksdocs/misc/evprev/ch3.htm. Accessed February 15, 2012.

"Purpose of the Washington Association" and "Fort Nonsense." *Washington Association of New Jersey.* http://wanj.org. Accessed May 20, 2015.

"Revolutionary War Signal Beacon Probably Located Atop Mount Bethel." *Warren Township Historical Society.* http://www.warrennj.org/wths/pages/signalbc.htm. Accessed January 13, 2013.

"Southern Campaign of the American Revolution." *National Park Service, Cowpens National Battlefield.* http://www.nps.gov/cowp/historyculture/southerncampaign.htm. Accessed May 19, 2013.

"Stories from the Revolution." *National Park Service, the American Revolution* http://www.nps.gov/revwar/about_the_revolution/capsule_history.html. Accessed May 26, 2012.

"Yorktown Battlefield, History of the Siege." *National Park Service, Yorktown National Battlefield.* http://www.nps.gov/york/historyculture/history-of-the-siege.htm. Accessed May 2012.

CPSIA information can be obtained
at www.ICGtesting.com
Printed in the USA
LVOW05s1011171115

462949LV00004B/5/P